Helping Children to be Competent Learners

From Birth to Three

Ann Roberts and Avril Harpley

Routledge
Taylor & Francis Group

LONDON AND NEW YORK

First published 2007 by Routledge
2 Park Square, Milton Park, Abingdon, Oxon, OX14 4RN

Simultaneously published in the USA and Canada
by Routledge

270 Madison Ave, New York, NY 10016

Routledge is an imprint of the Taylor & Francis Group, an informa business

Typeset in Trade Gothic by FiSH Books, Enfield, Middx.
Printed and bound in Great Britain by TJ International Ltd, Padstow

British Library Cataloguing in Publication Data
A catalogue record for this book is available from the British Library.

Library of Congress Cataloging in Publication Data
A catalogue record for this book has been requested.

ISBN 10: 1-84312-450-5
ISBN 13: 978-1-84312-450-4

Contents

Acknowledgements

We would like to thank the following children and parents who provided some wonderful photographs to be used in this book:

Mark Williams; Childminder, Lewisham, London
Laura Henry; Early Years consultant – Childcare consultancy
Anna and Eve, and their parents Gregory and Cath
Poppy and her parents Mick and Leanne, and Grandma Sandra
Lucas and Jago and their parents Debbie and Chris
Alison Cobb; St Albans, Herts
The parents of Katie and her brother Mathew
Molly and her granddad. Sisters Kaisha and Fraiyah.

Warm thanks also to the many friends and colleagues who have helped to test run the practical activities.

Ann and Avril

Introduction

Helping children to become competent learners can provide them with a positive disposition for lifelong learning and be the catalyst in germinating the seed that is their potential. The early years from 0 to 3 are a unique period in a young child's life as he encounters experiences for the very first time. It can be a confusing, even chaotic time, when he is trying to make sense of the world, testing out ideas, making connections and discovering how and where he fits in. Young children are naturally curious, inquisitive, they like to explore and experiment and in this way, they make their own discoveries and draw conclusions.

Everything a child experiences has a direct influence on the development of the brain and the emotions. Throughout life learning is the process of adjusting information and knowledge, changing one set of beliefs and concepts in the light of new discoveries. Initially learning is through the senses and is mainly physical and practical, or 'hands on'. It is active, playful and is strengthened by the emerging interaction with their peers and significant adults. Later, children develop the impulse to record their experiences through representation and language. To the untrained eye early mark making appears to be random scribbles and lines but they represent a child's inner drive and intention, a need to record feelings and experiences. These marks develop into forms of communication that encompass symbols and drawings. Children observe the behaviour of adults and their peers. They imitate what they see and learn as they re-enact familiar situations during role play yet have the security of being able to maintain control of the outcome.

This book uses the framework of *Birth to Three Matters* (DfES, 2002) and adds to it some effective everyday suggestions of activities which parents and carers can try with their baby or toddler. Every child is unique and some children develop their speech at different rates. Adults need to act as interested enablers and through acknowledging and encouraging children they will engender confidence. These are the intentions behind the activities and suggestions for children.

In this book the activities are based around easily accessible everyday items in order to encourage practitioners to use these objects to support and reflect the home environment within the setting. Simple role-play opportunities, such as using boxes and cloths, encourage open-ended play and exploration, enabling children to communicate what is in their mind. Imagination, creativity and language are all interconnected.

By posing challenges and questions to staff, readers are invited to reflect on their own practice and think about how they can communicate more effectively with babies and toddlers and assist their developing skills.

Why should we help children to become competent learners?

The purpose of this book is to help practitioners consider ways in which they can provide support and encourage babies and young children to become competent learners. There are four sections: making connections, representing, being creative and being imaginative. These refer to the government's *Birth to Three Matters* guidelines.

The quality of the adults who work with young children and babies is key to their successful development. They too need to be competent learners who are committed to professional development and open to ideas. Working with babies and young children is an area where the adult observes and follows rather than leads and directs. In this way, activities are initiated by the interests of the child and developed by the skill of the practitioner. Their role demands that they are both carers and educators who have to take into account the safety and protection of the children. Yet this should not prevent them from providing rich and varied experiences within a stimulating and inviting environment, both indoors and outdoors.

A sensitive practitioner recognises that young children need to be independent, at times insisting on doing things for themselves yet at other times needing support, encouragement and reassurance.

> Never let a child risk failure until he has a reasonable chance of success.
>
> (Dr Maria Montessori, www.montessori.org.uk/MMQuotations.php)

Effective practitioners develop respectful two-way relationships with parents and carers. In their role as significant adults, they have to be non-judgemental and without prejudice as they may have a profound influence over what the children in their care value and believe. They have a unique opportunity to help each child develop his learning potential and be confident as an individual.

How to use this book

This book has been written with a practical focus in mind. Practitioners need ideas to use with babies and toddlers. They are busy people and have limited resources at their disposal. The connections made with *Birth to Three Matters* at the beginning of each chapter are designed to support them as they plan and use the documents on a daily basis.

After an introduction, each chapter contains six numbered parts, each one subdivided into sections. The first two sections of each part look at babies and toddlers. The baby section covers from 0 to 18 months and the toddlers' section runs from 18 to 36 months. Both provide practical activities. Obviously, the practitioner will recognise that every child is unique and so adaptations to some of the suggested activities will be necessary. Safety is very important and so cautionary advice is offered throughout the book. If children have specialist needs, readers will need to take these into consideration before using the activities and make an informed safety decision on how to use them in their situation.

Following the activities is a section on the outcomes for the child. The points are designed to help us fully recognise the importance of the child in everything that is offered. If we are intending to help children to become competent learners, we need to assess how well we are doing this from the child's point of view. Ofsted also focuses on this within its inspection framework and so this will assist the practitioners in their evaluations and their preparation for an Ofsted visit.

The focus points that follow are to make us as adults draw some thoughts and feelings together about the practical activities, their purpose, the impact they have and how this can all be built on for the child. They are intended to encourage the reader to consider, question and reflect.

Staff discussion is important. Talking about what we do and trying to make sense of it with others helps us to improve the quality and standard of our work. If we want children to become competent learners, we need to see how our role is fitting into the overall picture and how effective we are being.

Finally, each chapter concludes with a list of references. These references are linked to three key documents: *National Standards for Under 8s Day Care and Childminding (Full Day Care)* (DfES/DWP, 2003), *Birth to Three Matters* (DfES, 2002) and *Every Child Matters* (DfES, 2003). These are intended to assist the reader in making connections between practice and theory. Chapters 3 and 4 also provide a list of resources which include related books and websites that practitioners might find useful.

References

DfES (Department for Education and Skills) (2002) *Birth to Three Matters: A Framework to Support Children in their Earliest Years.* London: DfES.

DfES (Department for Education and Skills) (2003) *Every Child Matters.* London: DfES.

DfES (Department for Education and Skills)/DWP (Department for Work and Pensions) (2003) *National Standards for Under 8s Day Care and Childminding (Full Day Care).* London: DfES.

Making connections

Introduction

As practitioners can we ever measure the consequences of our involvement with children? Probably not. We are only a part of the many influences working around a child that include the family, culture, the environment, society, politics and opportunities. Children do not enter a setting brand spanking new, gift wrapped, equal and ready to go. However, as Jean Piaget commented, children are born with a drive to make sense of the world.

The components in the *Birth to Three Matters* guidelines for 'A Competent Learner' link the experiences that every child needs: social, emotional, physical, intellectual and creative. Children want to explore, investigate, experiment, interact with each other and adults, ask questions, solve problems, use their imagination and represent. To do this they need support and encouragement from skilled adults who know when to jump in and when to stand back.

These early experiences have a real impact on the brain: they affect how the brain is wired and can influence future attitudes and capabilities. A critical part of our role is to help to develop children's learning potential, build on their natural curiosity and desire to make sense of the world. By providing quality opportunities for first-hand experiences, handling materials and objects, they are able to make connections and develop abstract concepts. The brain stores information in thousands of individual dendrites that resemble the branches of a tree. A rich environment increases the growth of dendrites. When a child sees and tastes his first apple he starts up a long-term file on apples and then as he learns more about apples, he creates associated files. For example, not all apples are the same; those that are green, red, golden or speckled we might store in our colour file, their round shape may be associated with other round objects such as oranges and footballs. The brain stores information in different areas: visual information, rhythm and music prefer to be stored in the right-hand side of the brain whereas verbal input, time, sequence, language and word processing tend to be stored in the left. Young children have in-built bodily memory – it is through repetitive movements that the muscles in their body learn to walk, run and ride a bike.

Since the mid-1990s there have been exciting developments in the understanding of the way children learn. Supporting schemas are seen as a powerful force and provide the most powerful tool for learning where children practise their ideas in a safe environment and consolidate new skills, concepts and thinking. Their thinking is represented through modelling, drawing, painting and role play.

> Knowledge can be acquired without having the disposition to use it.
>
> (Katz, 1993)

A critical part of the practitioner's role with young children is to foster a positive attitude towards learning. Some children may have the skills to read but lack the disposition to do so. Just because they can doesn't mean they will or want to. However, if the practitioner shows visible and positive signs of enjoying reading, the child may wish to imitate them. Enjoyment is not the goal – enjoyment is for entertainers; however, learning should engage the mind of the learner and be a pleasurable and rewarding experience.

1. Connecting ideas and understanding about the world

Young children learn through repeating patterns of play (sometimes called SCHEMA).

(*Birth to Three Matters*)

Babies

Observing how a baby crawls and the repeated patterns she makes as she begins to gain confidence illustrates that babies use repetition to enhance well-being and to consolidate what they are learning about their world. Throwing toys down can be linked to a pattern of schema called the trajectory scheme, whereas repeating circular movements in various ways could indicate or link eventually to a radial schema. However, identifying any patterns of play requires observations skills and knowledge of schemas themselves.

Practical activities

- Use a collection of bowls and spoons to encourage stirring round and round.
- Use natural objects, such as butter squash and gourds, which create different patterns of movement and allow crawling and moving after them.
- Use circular mats with circular items on and observe the patterns of play.
- Thread objects such as CDs along a line of ribbon or string so that they can be physically moved back and forward to support schemas.
- Lay out a series of exercise mats on the floor so that babies can crawl backwards and forwards.
- Make a collection of toys that roll and give babies the space to explore them.
- Make simple trails using laminated pictures or simple placemats (the large fruit pictures variety) sealed on the floor, some in circles and some in lines.

Toddlers

Young children systematically explore aspects of their world through abstract ideas such as verticality, connection, transporting and enveloping. These activities link apparently random activities together. They discover many different ways to work through their theme such as expressing it in painting, role play, and construction or asking for favourite stories that embody the schema ideas. When the witch puts Hansel and Gretel in the oven it feeds a child's enveloping or enclosing schema. It has been suggested that if certain schemas, such as enclosure, are not worked through, abstract concepts such as area or volume are not so easily understood.

Below are a few ideas to support some of the common schemas.

Practical activities

- Transporting. Provide a collection of objects together with buckets, bags, baskets and trucks so that children can transport them from place to place and back again.

- Enveloping. Children will want to cover themselves and objects with material, paint, even glue. Make available cloths, wrapping paper, boxes with lids, hats and dressing-up clothes, materials for making dens. Find stories to read where characters are wrapped up cosy in bed, climb into things, wear different clothes. This schema can often be recognised when a child paints a picture then covers it over entirely with a layer of colour.

- Connecting. This schema shows itself when children want to link, connect or tie things together. They will be drawn to Lego bricks, train tracks and carriages, trucks with trailers, bikes and trailers, tying string and ribbons. In addition you can play games where children hold hands or hold on to each other's waists.

- Ordering. The classic example of this schema is the story of the 'Three bears'. Children will enjoy putting toy animals into enclosures, arranging them in size, lining up the bikes and later ordering pictures into a logical sequence.

Outcomes for the child

- Motivation to explore and express ideas and concepts.
- Better understanding of the world.

Focus points

To observe a schema try to look beyond the obvious activity and discover the thread that underlies it. Schemas do not appear in any specific order, they do not follow a developmental stage; however, they are easily recognisable in younger children. Sometimes a child may be exploring two different schemas at the same time; often he will join up with another child and play with him while they share the same schema.

Note: schema spotting takes time and this can be a useful project to do as a team, discussing ideas as you go.

Staff discussion

- Observe children during free play and note their schema. Discuss with staff if other children have the same one and make provision to support. For example, if vertical or horizontal schemas are being explored, provide torches to shine straight lines, blocks to build towers, construction equipment, rail tracks, grids or aeroplane toys. Their independent mark making may show examples of vertical and horizontal lines and letters such as T, H, L, I or X.

- Talk with parents/carers to find out if a schema is evident at home. For example, is their child exploring covering everything up or tying objects together?

2. Connecting through the senses and movement

Young babies use movement and sensory exploration to connect with their immediate environment.

(*Birth to Three Matters*)

Babies

Babies' early movements begin with stretching and extending out into their new world. Once they are mobile, their crawling movements tend to be forward and in a linear pattern. Going upstairs is much easier than coming down, moving forward is easier than backwards. Different bodily techniques are used. They crawl and explore their world using touch as a key sense. They also follow circular patterns and this can be found in early mark-making 'scribbles'. Moving allows connections to happen and learning to begin.

Practical activities

- Collect items that roll in different directions, and if possible, use natural materials such as gourds or butter squash. These create haphazard movements and challenge movement patterns. This combines the sense of sight and movement stimulation.

- Choose some simple black and white pictures and laminate them. Place them on the floor in different pattern trails, swapping between straight lines and curves for variety.

- Use a circular mat and a circular basket with items in it which can roll and, if possible, have sounds in such as sound balls (unused cat toys/collars are good for this but check for safety!) or musical instruments. Combine sound and movement.

- Collate some songs that have related movements, such as 'Round and round the garden' – linking the sense of touch and movement.

Toddlers

Toddlers reach a stage where they wish to be independent – the 'me do it' time. It can get messy when they explore paint, dough, sand and water; however, a crucial part of learning is being able to handle new materials freely, finding out how they work and what they can do with them. There is often a spurt in learning followed by a lull, while the body and the mind adjust to the new learning. You will find that some children will want to repeat activities many times just for enjoyment but also to master a skill. They need encouragement to show approval and to build up self-esteem and confidence.

Practical activities

- Finger and toe painting. Use wallpaper lining paper so that the children can walk along in their bare feet, covered in paint. Ensure you have a bowl of water and a towel nearby for those children who dislike being 'messy'. Different forms of mark making help to develop hand–eye co-ordination. Hand and feet printing connects mark making with language/symbols.

- Dancing with ribbons and scarves helps a toddler to use larger arm movements and gain better control.

- Spinning and circle play. Place ropes on the ground in a spiral shape for children to walk upon or beside. Encourage spinning, twirling and circle games. Current research suggests that this helps brain development and balance.

- Provide a variety of construction toys that have to be pushed together and pulled apart. Have sponges in the water tray to squeeze and dough that can be pulled, stretched, rolled and kneaded to make shapes. These activities will develop muscles in the wrists and hands.

- Trying to capture a slippery ice-cube in the water tray and having fun in a fluid environment also helps to strengthen hands and fingers. Provide tip and pour activities with different sized bottles and funnels. A household sieve will make a shower of water to trickle gently over arms and hands.

Outcomes for the child

- Learning and senses are seamlessly integrated.
- Learning experiences are linked to first-hand investigations.
- Development of hand–eye co-ordination and strengthening of muscles.

Focus points

Once a baby is around six months old she is able to sit up and take an interest in the world. The trunk or core of the body develops first, then she can control her arms and legs and later fingers and toes.

By two and a half she can engage in energetic play, run, dance, spin and stretch using all of her body.

Planned activities should focus on movement and learning in the early years. Consider the level of movement available when presenting activities.

Caution: Inquisitive babies and toddlers find and pick up the most amazing and often very small objects. Monitor their discoveries carefully. Be aware of cushions, pillows that could smother a young baby and ribbons and cords that could get caught in fingers and toes. Double check the size of objects that might be mouthed or swallowed and choke a baby.

Staff discussion

- How much space do we allow children to have between activities such as in a baby room? Encouraging physical movement from activity to activity needs to be evaluated – too far and a child may not attempt it; too close and it may be overwhelming. Discuss room layouts.

3. Finding out about the environment and other people

As they become more mobile, babies connect with toys, objects and a wider group of people.

(Birth to Three Matters)

Babies

Once mobility occurs, the view of the world experienced by a baby on her tummy – which is about 9 inches in height – increases. Crawling and walking increases her levels of vision and the distance of the exploration area. Even venturing out in a buggy and/or a car seat extends the environment.

Other people's faces begin to fascinate babies as well as their own reflections in mirrors. Once mobility develops connections begin to expand and their purpose and involvement with toys changes. The world a baby operates in is growing and presents new challenges; experiences of meeting new people and discovering new objects. She learns to connect with them and understand what they can do.

Adults need to be sensible and recognise that even young babies have likes and dislikes. Not all babies like balloons or clowns for instance. They find them very frightening. It is important to observe and monitor areas of apprehension and discuss them to establish a possible source or reason. If a child gets distressed over something, it is important that the staff team know and respect this.

Practical activities

- Collect photographs of faces and put them in a photo album. Include the babies' parents/carers if possible – if black and white pictures are used, it will be easier for the baby to recognise her loved ones.

- Make a montage of faces with old and young people from different races and laminate it. Include the pictures of the babies in the room and the key workers. Put these on a low level where the babies crawl and can look at them.

- The environment must include the outside – the babies need to experience the outside world. Ensure that they have warm clothing and also effective protection on hot days so they can experience the outdoors. Put up mirrors, at buggy height, so that they can go out and be pushed along and see, hear and touch things. Plan a baby sensory area.

- A baby's environment should be at different levels – some floor and tummy time, seated time or crawl/walk time as well as some different surfaces. Their environment is as imaginative as that of others who play with them.

Toddlers

A child who is able to relate easily to others and can communicate clearly has a better chance of having his needs met and will develop positive relationships in the future. Social competence develops from experiencing positive interactions and the knowledge that others are caring and supportive. However, those children who have had the experience that the world is a frightening place and that adults cannot be trusted will need a very sensitive and caring approach. In order to feel confident enough to explore the wider world children need to make strong bonds with significant adults who they can trust, have an awareness of others' feelings, be able to say 'no' and take the initiative. They need to develop acceptable behaviour through an awareness of, and an ability to adjust to, social conventions and expectations.

Practical activities

- Provide regular outdoor play and activities so that the children can experience the natural world and the elements first hand: feeling the wind, the rain and the sun, smelling the earth after rain and listening to the sounds around them. In this way they will begin to learn about the changing seasons, birds and butterflies, observe the growth and decay of plants.

Caution: Make sure the children have suitable clothing and some spares to change into if they get wet or dirty.

- Explore ways to widen children's understanding of the wider world by introducing a variety of visitors to the setting. These may include local tradespeople or workers within the community such as the fire, police and ambulance services or family members who wish to share experiences with the children. Prepare the visits carefully and introduce the visitor and his/her reasons for visiting. Teach the children the social conventions of polite behaviour and greeting. Build up a collection of photographs and videos together with songs and music that show the diversity of race, culture and lifestyle within the community.

- Ensure that children are aware of the safe boundaries within the setting and outside. Walk with them and point these out. Create a road safety game with traffic cones; teach the symbols, signs and awareness of traffic for safer crossings.

- Select a soft toy as a special friend that can be taken home by children for 'sleepovers'. Encourage families to include this toy in their daily life, their holidays and outings, taking photos and keeping a diary. Later, on their return to the setting, ask the children to share these experiences with the group. Extend this activity by keeping a simple map of the local area, or if appropriate, the wider world, to plot the journeys the toy has made.

- Provide equipment that allows the children to examine the world from different viewpoints such as digital microscopes, magnifying lenses or telescopes. Let them discover where different mini beasts live, how they move and what they eat.

Outcomes for the child

- Children understand their world and how far it extends.
- Growing awareness of nature and the changing seasons.
- Increased confidence and more secure relationships.

Focus points

Regular outdoor play is an essential part of a young child's development; however, if outdoor space is limited, explore possibilities of visiting local parks or woodland, organise walks around the block or contact local schools to see if you can share their playing field.

Sensitive adults will anticipate situations that could prove difficult for shy, reserved children by allowing them to take their time, stay close to a significant adult and prompt them gently to initiate being friendly and joining in with others. Those children who have suffered from multiple transitions from an early age may find it difficult to trust a new carer or stranger; they have already experienced lost friendships. They need very careful preparation for change.

Staff discussion

- Do you have sufficient suitable clothing available for children to play outside, whatever the weather?
- Do staff provide positive role models for social interactions?
- Are there simple rules to encourage good behaviour, politeness and good manners?
- Do you have strategies to help new children become integrated into the group?
- Are there clear, simple rules for security, limits and boundaries?

4. Playfully engaged and involved

Follow personal interests and make connections.

(Birth to Three Matters)

Babies

Babies are unique beings and are little people in their own right. Their interests grow and develop day by day. They are beginning to build up their personality and interest from very early on and when a group of babies are together this becomes noticeable, certainly to an astute key person who spends time with them. It is important to establish their interests as with older children – it is only then that you can communicate, provide and encourage growth with true understanding. Providing a stimulating and varied environment and observing the responses of individual babies will help to gather evidence of interests and see connections actually happening.

Practical activities

- Once you have spotted a key interest provide a small treasure basket with a lid on it. Put a photograph on this to denote which baby it belongs to. Place inside a collection of things she connects with.

- With the help of parental information build on interests and provide photographs and new artefacts to develop them.

- Provide resources such as lengths of voile and netting cloths for child to play and make their own connections from.

- Provide large tubes and cylinders and allow babies to engage in their chosen way of playing in a free floor space.

- Collect photos when children engage in their own individual interests. This has purpose and provides information – it is when a baby is saying 'This is me!'

⚠ **Caution:** Always use mirrors made from toughened safety glass or acrylic.

- Provide new items to encourage new interests such as collections of mirrors and shiny items.

Toddlers

Play is a powerful tool for learning. It provides opportunities for social, emotional, intellectual and physical development. Play comes out of the mind of the player rather than the object he plays with. A child transforms the objects to be what he needs at the time. It allows him to construct meaning out of the everyday events in his life. Play brings the big wide world down to a size that a child can cope with and control or walk away from. In a playful situation a child can safely explore frightening ideas, thrilling and exciting games. During play a child will investigate, experiment, organise ideas, solve problems and develop relationships with his peers.

Practical activities

- Provide a wide variety of materials so that the children can construct dens, build landscapes in the sand tray or create underwater worlds in the water tray.

- Observe children role playing and extend the play by intervening and introducing a new event or materials. For example, the postman has delivered a letter with some exciting news, a magic seed has been discovered, a strange egg has appeared, there is an emergency and everyone is needed to help bandage and care for patients, a colourful mask brings in a new player.

- Observe role play and intervene by removing some of the equipment. For example, the play house cooker needs to be repaired – where can you get a plumber? The office photocopier won't work – what can you do? The mobile phone battery has run – down how can you get a message home? Allow the children to come up with problem-solving ideas.

- Set up an everyday happenings or a scenario. For example, Teddy has lost his 'comforter', one of the toy horses has broken a leg. What happens next? What should we do? Make sure resources include materials that reflect the real world so that children can act out their everyday lives: going to the shops, the hairdressers, the chippy, the garage or the car wash. Support play where they may need to act out fears or anxieties in a safe environment such as a visit to the dentist or the hospital.

- Provide a large cardboard box and watch what the children do with it. You can cut holes for windows or doors, paint it, add buttons for the push-button controls of an aeroplane or rocket.

- Create fantasy dens, for example under the sea, at the North Pole, in a jungle. Add to the atmosphere with coloured lights, sound effects and music. Let the children use small world animals and objects to create scenarios and then photograph them, add text to the pictures and create their own story books.

Outcomes for the child

- Children feel they can be individual and have personal interests.
- Children are empowered and have control over the play.
- Play can meet a child's needs – social, emotional, cultural, intellectual and physical.
- During play a child can learn at his own level and interest.

Focus points

Sometimes we plan activities for children that may not be what the children are interested in or even need. The saying 'one size fits all' is not appropriate. We need to watch, listen and learn, observe the things the children explore, what they construct or draw in order to tune in to their current interests. Observation of children during their play is crucial and shows us how they are experimenting and trying out ideas, interacting with each other and using their imagination as they try to make sense of the world. It helps us to follow their lead, support and encourage their efforts by supplying the right resources and materials. Positive playful situations allow children to make connections between the present and previous experiences and to develop mastery over materials and manipulative skills. It is during play that children practise skills or develop new ones.

Staff discussion

- In a group perhaps one or two children do not display specific interests as clearly as others. How can we tease this out?
- Could we follow an interest as part of our overall plan – or use this collection of interests as the vision for our planned activities much more?
- Do you employ effective methods to get to know the children, their families, any life-changing events that might be taking place?
- Do you join in with children's play, have fun and relax with them?

5. Making patterns, comparing, categorising, classifying

Provide stimulating materials for young children to match, sort, classify and categorise.

(*Birth to Three Matters*)

Babies

Babies use all their senses to explore. As they mouth objects they discover the qualities of taste and texture. They respond to familiar sounds and faces and link them with pleasurable experiences. Hands and feet discover that some objects slip, fall and roll and then, when they are more mobile, they can make these things happen themselves, pushing, pulling and throwing. Piaget describes this as sensori-motor exploration.

By providing collections of similar items and different unexplored objects their curiosity and brain power will be extended.

Practical activities

● Simple posting boxes encourage babies to match up and test out their spatial awareness. Have a variety of these but recognise that babies often want to repeat an action and use the same toy over and over again. Babies love to put items in and out of containers and by carefully selecting the objects you can start them sorting and classifying early by ensuring only specific things fit into some places.

● Treasure baskets are merely collections of objects. Collect things that are the same – for example, collect items made of wood and use as a single collection to be explored in full and then introduce a new collection, for instance metal or shiny objects.

● Use simple items to start classifications – a tea set with two settings for example. Remember the attributes that adults use for classifying may not be the same for babies or young children. Talk with them to find out why they have chosen to put items together.

● Ensure that baskets, boxes and containers are available frequently for free play as this facilitates early sorting opportunities.

Toddlers

Sorting, grouping and classifying objects will help children to understand the relationships between them. Toddlers enjoy making collections and will usually sort according to one attribute, the quality or property of the object. They may include or reject items for collections if they have the same attribute or are different. Some items may have only one attribute in common that causes a relationship, for example they are all wooden, all shiny, and all small. Young children can only focus on one attribute at a time; however, as they develop they will be able to describe two or more attributes, although when using the material they will keep only one uppermost. Children who have had a great deal of experience in sorting, classifying, ordering and working out relationships between objects and materials will be forging a good foundation for mathematics.

Practical activities

- Go outside and allow children time to look for items to collect. Give them a small container. On return indoors provide clear sticky back paper or empty CD boxes so that they can select and fix their treasure to keep or display. Encourage them to talk about why they have chosen and included the items. Ask them to describe them, wonder what they are for, and create labels for them noting their special qualities. Take note of the attributes that attract each child.

- Use computer software programs that help children recognise and create shapes. Provide three-dimensional resources so that the children can recreate the designs using bricks and blocks. Photograph their constructions. Have paper shapes or collage materials available so that the children can design further patterns and shapes.

- Equip boxes with play materials that go together, for example things for the kitchen, cutlery trays for knives, forks and spoons, tools for play dough, a collection of green items, large and small dinosaurs. Some of these will be the same, others not the same. Observe how the children sort them.

- Hide a selection of toy snakes in the sand tray; include some identical pairs and ask the children to find them and sort them. Observe how they select and sort the snakes.

- Observe the children as they play and note if they are using linear or circular schemas. Encourage the children to explore making linear and circle shapes during dance and movement. Introduce traditional and modern dances where children dance in a line or in a circle. Provide coloured pegs to create washing line patterns or small toy animals that can be lined up.

Outcomes for the child

- Developing simple lifting, holding and dropping skills.
- Developing observation skills, linking ideas.
- Organising information by comparing, classifying and describing attributes.

Focus points

Think about how in your own life you need the skills of sorting and classifying and how important they are.

They help to make sense of the world and create effective organisation. Consider the resources you use with babies and toddlers. Do you have a wide variety, are there sufficient to give choice, are there too many? How do you present the resources? Are they laid out invitingly, in specific, well-ordered piles or in a heap? How do children react? Think about reasons for purposely combining resources and presenting them in a new or different ways.

Staff discussion

- Review your resources to include a wide variety of interesting objects for sorting and classifying. Collect objects from the natural world such as colourful shells, oddly shaped stones. Introduce old mechanical objects such as clock parts, fabrics with different textures (silky, rough, etc.), patterns and colours.
- Supply sorting boxes, divided dishes or baskets to sort them into.
- Provide good, accessible storage so that collections can be kept. Label the storage with digital photographs of the contents to help children return them easily.

6. Connecting ideas and understanding the world

For some children the world is their home language, family and street.

(Birth to Three Matters)

Babies

The world is a complex place for children and they are shaped by their personal experiences and family environment. Many homes have cultural and religious influences which are a key focus in their day-to-day lives and this will affect how their babies see and experience the world. Having respect and regard for these is important in the partnership work that should be going on with the parents/carers and the setting. Babies may be fed or held in a certain way or at certain times there are routines which are upheld. Connecting ideas and understanding the world may require appreciation of others and their world, offering experiences that are wide and open ended and not judgemental. A baby's world can be a variable place, where people come and go. They may be with a grandparent, childminder, friend as well as in a setting within a single day – never mind in a week. Making positive connections with families will help staff to help the babies make sense of the world.

Practical activities

- Have artefacts and resources that are multicultural. Make a treasure basket in which you put various items from their culture so that they can see familiar objects.

- Avoid tokenism – by all means celebrate festivals but remember cultures and religions are here in the environment all year round. Colouring in printouts for festivals means nothing to a baby. Look beyond the physical activity and evaluate what is being learnt from it.

- Encourage different fruits and foods in snack time. The backgrounds that many children are coming from are rich in diversity so reflect this in their daily experiences.

- Present resources in different ways and allow children time to connect with them – for example, using different sizes and shapes of spoons with imaginative play, in the sand, water or gloop as well as when we eat.

Toddlers

An early years setting needs to take on board all aspects of equal opportunity for every child whether it is related to gender, culture or religion and operate a fully inclusive setting. A basic instinct is to reject what we don't understand – we are generally frightened of the unfamiliar. Fear and ignorance go hand in hand so it is important that staff develop young children's knowledge and understanding of the wider world. Children can be shown that one way is not necessarily better or worse than another, just different.

Children need approval, to be liked, make friends and asked around to tea. At this age, it is far more important to be accepted by your peers than learning phonics and numbers. Without good feelings about themselves, learning can be difficult. Adults should aim to present a world in which both sexes, young and old from all cultural and ethnic backgrounds, have positive qualities and are capable of dominating the action. No mean task!

Practical activities

- Encourage children to share their experiences of special times throughout the year; the food they eat, any special diets, the clothes they wear and the gifts they receive. Replicate aspects of these experiences in pretend play or with small world toys and support the children to represent them through art and craft.

- Build up a resource of world music and encourage the children to play the tapes freely.

- Provide digital video recorders, PDAs (personal digital assistants), digital cameras or audio tapes so that children and their families can record aspects of their family life and share these with the group.

- Have full-length safety mirrors where the children can see themselves. Encourage them to paint or make models of themselves.

- Display positive visual images of both sexes, of ethnic groups and people with disabilities (for example, a wheelchair marathon).

- Collect patterns, fabrics and artefacts from around the world. Do they tell a story?

- Create a Caribbean picnic under an umbrella complete with food tasting, reggae music and posters of beaches. Try out hairstyles, braids and beads.

> **Caution:** Limit salt and salty products and sugar. Be aware that nuts can cause choking in young children. Check additives and E numbers on processed foods and biscuits.

Outcomes for the child

- Consistency for the child – feeling safe in his world.

- Respect and understanding about his world supports well-being and confidence.

- Developing a feeling of belonging.

Focus points

Connecting with a wider world is about developing positive attitudes as well as provision. Children learn through and from their immediate environment and the people close to them. Once learnt these feelings are hard to change. They absorb the values and beliefs held by significant adults and this will shape their own for the future. Often feelings about gender, ethnicity, ability or disability are deeply held, deeply rooted and adults may behave unconsciously, unaware of any partiality. The younger the children are in your care, the more you need to worry about their feelings and the greater your role in helping them to develop a sense of belonging and positive self-esteem that will help them to reach their full potential. Recognising needs is one element, but ensuring equality is reached is another. Review current policies and their effectiveness, ensure that they are put into practice and staff are positive role models, walking the talk.

Consider how the staff can use their talents and skills. Is there is a diversity among the staff team which is rich in human experience and resources? Discover the whole world of the child and then you can understand how and what he connects with and most importantly why.

Staff discussion

- Understanding a child's world today is not easy. Having an insight into his background can help. Consider home visiting or time allocated to spend with parents/carers. If an interpreter is needed, try to do this and ensure there is equality of access and opportunity.

- Staff need to look at how they communicate care and education to the outside world. Parents/carers may have widely differing expectations, and ideas that refer back to the experiences they had as a child. Providing this understanding and communicating it in this way can make the babies'/toddlers' world more connected.

- Review resources – stories, songs, rhymes and music – regularly and update. What images are portrayed, how are the characters shown, are the boys all active and the girls passive? Are there images of ethnic minorities, different landscapes, different countries? Providing toys and artefacts from different cultures can help children make the connection between the familiar home and their setting and therefore feel more secure.

- When talking with the children be aware of whom you address questions to, give tasks to, have jokes with, encourage gently or discipline more firmly.

References

Athey, C. (1990) *Extending Thought in Young Children*. London: Paul Chapman Publishing.

Bowlby, J. (1953) *Child Care and the Growth of Love*. London: Penguin.

DfEE (Department for Education and Employment)/QCA (Qualifications and Curriculum Authority) (2000) *Curriculum Guidance for the Foundation Stage: Personal, Social and Emotional Development*. London: DfES/QCA.

DfES (Department for Education and Skills) (2002) *Birth to Three Matters: A Framework to Support Children in their Earliest Years*. London: DfES.

DfES (Department for Education and Skills) (2003) *Every Child Matters*. London: DfES.

DfES (Department for Education and Skills)/DWP (Department for Work and Pensions) (2003) *National Standards for Under 8s Day Care and Childminding (Full Day Care)*. London: DfES.

Katz, L. G. (1993) 'Dispositions as educational goals', *ERIC Digest*. Champaign, IL: ERIC Clearinghouse on Elementary and Early Childhood Education (ERIC Document No. ED363454) (www.ericdigests.org/1994/goals.htm).

Nutbrown, C. (1984) *Threads of Thinking*. London: Paul Chapman Publishing.

2 Representing

Introduction

Representing is a very important experience for a child. It is a way of expressing and sharing his feelings and emotions. Many parents treasure their child's first fingerprints or footprints as they are unique and represent a milestone in development. Being able to preserve ideas and share them with others through representation is a lifelong experience. In some cultures symbols and marks are respected with great reverence.

Adults need to show children that they value and appreciate their mark making and prints. Scribbling, sometimes seen as a nuisance by parents and practitioners, is an essential stage of development that children experience in order to practise and establish their hand–eye co-ordination skills while they gain an understanding about representing their ideas at a two-dimensional level. This can be seen as a clear development from babies' early marks using their tiny fingers in milk to toddlers making a single recognisable letter of their name.

A wide range of opportunities can be offered that turn these early explorations into exciting and vibrant activities that are both satisfying and great fun. Colouring in a picture pre-prepared by an adult is of little value and is certainly not a record of a unique and personal piece of work.

More recently we have seen a development of tools and resources that fit the small hands and wrists of babies and toddlers who are just developing the muscles to grasp and hold materials. Kitchen shops are producing small spoons and brushes which are for the specialist but also ideal for little people when they explore the exciting world of paint, sand and water.

The local high street is a place full of signs and symbols where toddlers can see colourful representations and understand their significance. They quickly pick this up in their everyday experiences and can soon identify specific brands in supermarkets, recognise fast food shops and merchandising. Representation leads to preservation and provides onlookers with insight and evidence of young children's development as competent learners.

1. Experimenting

Exploring, experimenting and playing.

(*Birth to Three Matters*)

Babies

Babies explore the space they are in even inside the womb. Once they are born they have another new area (their new world) to explore which their senses pick up very quickly after their birth. Part of a baby's learning is experimenting, touching, feeling, mouthing to establish what objects are and trying to understand where they fit into their world.

Babies will explore faces and places. Babies experiment with new resources/toys they are offered. Playing can mean just watching and looking at their own hands and feet as well as interacting with specific resources on offer.

Messy play is an important part of learning and even babies need this first-hand experience as they begin to make sense of the world. Sand, water, clay and dough all need to be presented carefully but are important materials in the natural world that need to be explored, experimented and played with.

Practical activities

- Collect together some unused dog toys and balls made of rubber. Rubber has a different, distinctive texture, smell and temperature. Present them to the baby in a treasure basket.

- Collect a variety or swatches of materials with different patterns, colours and textures and let them be explored, touched, placed in and out of the basket in which they are offered.

- Use play dough – make it using a cooked recipe with cornflour and several fruity teabags to give colour, flavour and texture. This dough has a different temperature as the cornflour content makes it feel cooler. Let babies pat, squeeze and poke it.

- Collect items that are transparent so that babies can hold them up and look through them. Place alongside some safety mirrors so they can experiment with colour and light early on in their development.

Toddlers

Play is an essential activity for young children as it helps them to unravel their world and make meaning out of their lives in ways that they can understand. During play they need to be able to experiment with a wide variety of materials, try them out, explore them, find out how they work and enjoy the experience for its own sake. They will often repeat activities many times, for example squashing dough, sifting sand, cutting out endless pieces of paper and spreading them with glue. This helps to develop their knowledge and understanding of the experience. Later they will be able to make a more informed choices and master techniques with confidence.

Practical activities

- Throughout the year, supply a range of seasonal fruits and vegetables. Encourage the children to handle them, smell and taste them. Support with photographs and posters or pictures of paintings by famous artists. Provide knives and forks, under careful supervision, and demonstrate how to cut the fruit and vegetables in different ways. Encourage the children to notice how the inside of an apple, for example, looks quite different from the outside.

- Use drama and physical activities. In order for the children to understand how a fish or a tortoise moves and behaves, they need good opportunities to observe them at close quarters, to ask questions and talk about them.

- Let the children decorate a shoe box that will become their own posting/receiving box and shows their own individuality. Provide glitter, felt tip pens, ribbons, cut outs, old postcards, seed packets for them to use. Finally, help them to create their own name label on the PC to print off and stick on. Arrange the boxes so that they are easily accessible for the children to use.

- Provide a range of resources to use in the sand or water tray so that children can play creating their own small worlds. Collect items from the natural world such as shells, stones, twigs, bark and mix with play people and toy animals.

- Introduce the children to an activity where they look at things from an unfamiliar viewpoint. Take a short walk around the environment, inside or out, and look from 'below or on top'. Take digital photographs and later ask the children if they can identify them.

- Set up real-life experiences, such as meeting the police, fire and hospital services and follow up with digital or video photos to recall the event. Use stories and opportunities to relive the experience through well-supported role play. Display photos of the children engaged in the role play.

Outcomes for the child

- Children become independent, self-confident and autonomous.
- Able to use their initiative and solve problems.
- Development of own unique identity.

Focus points

Young children learn by watching and imitating adults and each other. From their earliest days they learn how to hold a cup, wash their hands or turn on the television. These actions become more complex as their experiences of the world increase. They will explore experiences, sometimes just for pleasure or to develop mastery and may later recreate them through representations. During role play, they may imitate someone driving a car or pretend to be an aeroplane in the sky. These actions help them to build up an internal image of the action or event that later is brought out as a simple mark, a symbol or a picture. Each child will make a representation in his own unique way as a concrete form of self-expression. Play that is active and practical, based on real experiences, has many benefits and connects with all the senses, plus it includes physical, emotional, social and creative development.

Staff discussion

- Join in with children's play but do not direct the play. Observe how they imitate you and copy what you do with the materials.

- Check that your resources incorporate natural materials, textures and smells, pattern, sounds and objects from around the world as well as familiar everyday items. Audit them regularly to keep them fresh and interesting.

- Observe and note children's spontaneous play. As they learn to understand their world and what is important they will demonstrate their ability to react to situations, be co-operative and collaborate, solve problems, show initiative and creativity/imagination and reveal their attitudes and disposition.

2. Making marks

Responding to the world with marks and symbols . . . Exploring, experimenting, playing.

(*Birth to Three Matters*)

Babies

From quite early on in their life babies start to explore and realise that their fingers, hands and feet actually belong to them. As they experiment with these new 'tools' they discover that they can make marks, prints and impact on materials. Encountering textures and substances such as milk spilt on a high chair tray provides an opportunity to make marks in the most basic form. Babies may appear reticent at first to handle some materials as the temperature of some substances might be cold and this will affect their confidence. The more experiences they are offered, the more adventurous they become. If babies are not allowed to be messy at home, they may find the first few sessions unusual and strange and they will need extra time and support.

Practical activities

- Strip babies down to their nappies and cover the floor. Provide large sheets of paper and paint. Support and enable their first encounters, exploring the paint and enjoying the experience. End the session with a clean up using warm water.

- Allow babies to sit in fine sand or close to a shallow sand tray, so they can feel the sand on their feet and legs and explore with their hands. Observe if they repeat actions or make marks.

- Encourage the discovery of water – splashing, patting and swirling, making marks in water or on a surface. Sometimes add gentle bubbles or lavender oil to the water to provide a sensory experience.

- Introduce mushroom or potato brushes (found in kitchenware shops) as they are easier for a baby to hold in a palm and to grip. Let babies dab and pat them on a variety of materials such as paint, sand, water or dough.

Toddlers

A toddler will start to order his world through mark making and symbols, although to an adult's eye these marks may look like random lines and scribbles. He may also use toys, blocks and bricks, arranging and rearranging them to his satisfaction as he experiments with shapes and patterns. Some marks may be repeated over and over in drawings and paintings. Often drawing and painting represents traces of energy and emotions rather than objects – for example, the speed of a car going down a road might be shown by rapidly drawing a number of vertical lines across the page rather than the car itself.

Practical activities

- Provide a wide variety of mark-making materials and tools. Have ample resources available, including paper in different sizes, shapes and textures together with felt tip pens, crayons, chalks, etc. Make sure they are freely available and accessible.

- Toddlers will be developing finer manipulative control. Ensure they have the choice of thinner brushes, pencils and crayons and a range of interesting tools that make marks in modelling clay, play dough.

- Initiate a specific task, a prompt to get the children started on representing. For example, following an active, first-hand experience, a story, make believe or real-life event, encourage them to record this through mark making, designing or three-dimensional modelling. This helps to focus and recall the experience as well as exercising their thinking skills.

- Talk with the children about their pictures, the models they have made or their pretend play. Don't ask 'What is it, what are you doing?' but instead say 'Tell me about . . .' Allow time and space during the session for them to revisit their creations; ask if they want to change anything or add anything; encouraging them to extend their experience.

- Supply a wide variety of materials for 'Create and make' sessions. These can often be found from scrap/resource centres, or collected by parents. Let them explore the materials freely without adult input. However, they should be taught and supervised in the use of tools such as hole punches, sticky tape, scissors, staplers, bulldog clips.

- Use dance and music so that children can express their emotions and feelings through gestures and body movements. Build up an eclectic collection of music that includes a variety of rhythms, sounds and moods.

- Add a variety of objects for the children to use with malleable materials, such as feathers, buttons, shells, sticks. Sit alongside and share in the modelling. In this relaxed play they will also be learning about shape, size, weight and elasticity.

- Encourage children's efforts to draw on steamy windows, make swirls and patterns with a stick in mud or sand and experience the pleasure of exploring finger paints. Time outdoors allows them to make large chalk drawings on the concrete or use decorators' brushes with water on fences and walls. They will also be exploring and discovering aspects of early science.

Outcomes for the child

- Children use their senses to learn about the world.
- Developing the ability to externalise their thoughts.
- Making begins in infancy – babies can see they can make an impact.
- Creative satisfaction.

Focus points

Begin by looking at scribbles and notice when this develops into more recognisable figures. Remember that this circular movement is natural for European children but think about how Chinese children develop in their mark making as they use more vertical and horizontal marks. An important stage in a young child's development is when the human figure emerges in his drawing and painting. Initially this looks like a tadpole, an oval or circular shape with linear lines coming from it that represent arms and legs. From the outset, the human face has deep significance for a child. If we put too much pressure on a child too soon to conform to conventional writing or drawing, we could harm his natural development and confidence.

Staff discussion

- Collect examples of children's developing ability to represent their thoughts and feelings in all its forms and media: art, craft, dance, imagination and problem solving. Use staff meetings to look at the examples and develop an awareness of the signs that indicate how the children are developing and what interests them.
- Observe and listen carefully to children's talk as they work. Recognise and value their efforts by engaging in a conversation about it and discover what they are trying to express.
- Share these early representational experiences with parents. Emphasise the learning that is taking place – the lines, shapes and colour.

3. Using tools and resources

Provide tools that imprint texture and depth in clay, dough and wet sand.
(*Birth to Three Matters*)

Babies

Babies' sense of touch is finely tuned. They begin to explore with their feet and then use their mouth to examine any object they encounter. Initially a baby's grasp is not easily sustained so it is important to choose items carefully to ensure she can hold them. Patting, pressing and poking soft, malleable materials are all important techniques that lead on to later creative skills. Supervision is important at these times to ensure that, should a baby put clay or dough in her mouth, it can be quickly and safely removed.

Practical activities

● In order to develop a baby's wrist, hand and finger strength, collect a selection of items that can be squeezed and pressed, such as large 'duvet' pegs, serving tongs and press and response toys. Place them in a treasure basket and call this your 'squeeze and press me' basket. Change the items as the baby gains competence.

- Collect short-handled tools like wooden pastry cutters, short brushes, and salt spoons. Allow babies to explore them. Encourage them to pat, press, dab or smack the surface of clay or dough.

- Introduce items that will imprint easily into soft dough such as shells, string or keys. Encourage and support babies as they explore this experience.

- Pressing down to any depth will be hard initially – use soft fine sand and then change the consistency by making it slightly damp. Introduce large plastic construction pieces that can be easily pressed into the sand.

Toddlers

Young children will use anything to hand to make marks – they will swirl a stick in a puddle or mud, pop their finger into cake mix or finger paint, make large arm movements in the air or through the water in the water tray. However, it is important that they have access to, and the availability of, good quality tools and materials. Inevitably, as they experiment with paint and paper they will use a great deal of resources without producing any end products and they may make a mess. Initially their movements and marks appear to be random but gradually these develop into something intentional, though not necessarily recognisable.

Practical activities

- Use stories, music, poetry and early science experiments to promote stimulating experiences, awe and wonder – for example, the sensory feel of the extraordinary material created by mixing corn flour and water or the simple scientific experiment of mixing vinegar and bicarbonate of soda to make a mini volcano.

- Create a special story area where children can snuggle up and enter the world of the imagination as they listen to stories one to one or in a small group. Decorate with cushions, pictures and fairy lights.

- Allow the children the freedom to explore the tools and materials in their own way, so that they can create their own individual representations.

- Messy play has a very useful function: it allows the children to explore the consistency, texture and sensations of materials and helps them to begin to understand how different materials behave or can be mixed together. Give the children ample time for exploration. Provide deep trays with a range of materials such as sawdust, glue, porridge and

> **Caution:** During messy play activities, ensure there is no contact with known allergens. Chemicals in paint, glue or detergent could pose a problem. Be especially aware of any contact allergies such as eczema which could be made worse by some activities.

cooked spaghetti. Let the children mix them together as they wish and delight in the feel of it.

- Thick paint is easier to control than runny. Mix with non-fungicidal glue so that the children can stick things into it on paper or card. Add soapflakes or an interesting texture such as sparkles, sand, icing sugar or rice. Provide wide-toothed combs to make patterns in the paint as well as sponges and brushes.

- Use white plastic tablecloths or individual tea trays to paint on as these can be wiped clean and reused. Provide one colour in a squeezy bottle, then add a second colour and finally a white or a black. In this way, the children can enjoy swirling colours together and learn colour blending. If detergent is added to paint, it helps to avoid staining and makes cleaning up easier.

- Malleable materials provide good sensory experiences but also develop manipulative skills. They can be pinched, rolled, squashed and pulled. Tools can be pressed into them to make patterns and marks. Explore kitchen utensils for interesting tools.

  > ⚠️ **Caution:** Be aware of sharp points and safety.

- Show the children how they can copy and print their pictures using a computer, photocopier or scanner. Let them take a copy home and keep one in their assessment portfolio.

Outcomes for the child

- Engaging with unknown materials and enjoying the experience promotes confidence and well-being.
- Sand is therapeutic and calming.
- Through active exploration of materials, children will be stimulating their sensory awareness.
- Development of hand–eye co-ordination and fine manipulative skills.

Focus points

Emphasis should be on the experience rather than what the finished product looks like. Practitioners need to 'let go' and let the children enjoy being creative. There can be a tendency for adults to want children's work to be 'recognisable', yet this is detrimental to creative thinking and individual expression. It can also harm a child's self-confidence and self-worth so that he becomes dependent on an adult's input and ideas and is dissatisfied with his own attempts. It is important that children's early efforts are valued and praised.

Staff discussion

- Be prepared for children to make a mess when exploring materials. Organise their messy play area so that with a minimum of fuss it can be cleaned and tidied up. Encourage the children to learn where to put rubbish, find a cloth, wash and dry their hands. Have easy to put on and fasten protective clothing.

- Help children to become autonomous; establish simple routines for getting out and putting away equipment. Organise storage so that materials can be easily seen and identified, have matching pictures and labels. Use symbols to show where tools fit and provide a visual clue if something is missing. Have day-to-day mark-making equipment in a central spot.

- Invest in a drying rack or an expanding laundry rack where children's wet paintings can be left and later collected. Have sticky labels on hand to quickly identify each child's work and to add comments and date.

- Show you value children's creative work by displaying it attractively, named and annotated with their own comments. Provide some display areas at adult height but also others low down where the children can see their own work.

- Explore situations that will develop motor skills. Demonstrate how to hold tools correctly, to push, pull, squeeze or roll them.

4. Brush and paint

Observe the early marks babies and children make when given a crayon or brush for the first time.

(*Birth to Three Matters*)

Babies

Babies tap and dab on surfaces at an early stage. Introducing paint captures these very early motions and marks. When babies see that their fingers, hands or feet make marks on paper they begin to learn cause and effect. They experience tactile and sensory skills from touching the paint and feeling the sensation of it on their skin and in between their fingers or toes. Supplying a variety of painting surfaces provides a wider experience for the baby. Cut down old towels to make protective clothing, or if body painting is occurring, strip down to nappies and let them enjoy a nice bath afterwards.

Practical activities

- Use foil as a painting surface. The paints remain on the top of the shiny surface. It provides another texture to explore and experience.
- Small mushroom or potato scrubbing brushes (found in good kitchenware shops) can be held easily in the palm and give babies greater control.
- Add baby talcum powder or baby lotion to paint. This creates a different texture and smell that turns the painting experience into a multi-sensory activity.
- Use black sugar paper and baby powder to make prints and marks with. The talcum powder really shows all the detail of the finger and hands.

Toddlers

Toddlers' hand–eye co-ordination slowly begins to develop more control and becomes more precise. Their mark making may start to show recognisable shapes and details as they learn to use materials and tools. Through experimenting and adult support they can manipulate pencils, crayons and paint brushes; they learn to judge how much pressure to put on to make a line or draw a circle. Toddlers' initial attempts at painting may start with a scrubbing motion, pushing or pulling the brush across the paper as they enjoy the experience of overlaying colours and the result is a wet soggy picture. However, the experience is what is important, not the end product.

Practical activities

- Build up the skills of using painting tools by providing a wide variety of brushes in different sizes and shapes. Introduce foam paddle brushes, and sponges. Provide different materials to paint on, not just paper, and allow time just to experiment, explore and enjoy the experience.
- Provide just two colours of paint and encourage the children to create swirls, blobs and dabs as they mix the two together and create a new colour.

- Use different painting surfaces, for example an easel, flat tables, large sheets of paper attached onto outside walls and large decorators' brushes and rollers. Put a long length of paper on the ground where they can splash or dribble paint. Encourage a group painting.

- Consider the skills needed to use computer software drawing programs, controlling the mouse to collect the brush and colour. Print out the picture. Duplicate the drawing in another medium such as crayons, paint or coloured pencils. Compare the results.

- Use coloured lights and fairy lights to create an atmosphere in a role-play area. Cover torches with acetate and shine onto white paper or draw circles in the air. Explore the colours in a rainbow, bubbles, prisms and crystals. Talk about how the colours make them feel. Do they have favourite colours?

Outcomes for the child

- Increased control when using tools and resources.
- Awareness of colour, shape, textures, materials.
- Increased confidence.
- Opportunities for self-expression.

Focus points

This period of experimentation is valuable and sensitive encouragement will build up children's confidence and control. It is important to show interest and appreciation in their mark making. They need to be able to have the freedom and materials readily available to create a profusion of marks using a wide variety of tools and materials. Painting is both an expressive and an emotional experience – some children will create shapes and symbols while others are more dramatic and their pictures tell a story. In the beginning they enjoy using colour for its own sake so an elephant may be pink or purple rather than grey.

Staff discussion

- What are the learning opportunities in a mark-making or painting activity? Observe and identify the skills it will develop. For example, manipulation, social development, sharing ideas, co-operation, interaction, listening to each other and following directions, obeying instructions, imagination and creativity, independence, clearing up, taking turns, attention, watching and imitating, concentration and perseverance, discrimination – being able to compare and contrast, size, shape and colour.

- Do you allow children to revisit their drawing and painting so that they can add details or change it, or does it have to be finished in one activity?

- Do you explain to parents/carers the stages of learning inherent in representation so that they can appreciate their children's efforts and be aware of what to look for, for example the development of a circle shape or an emerging human figure?

- Look for schemas that appear in painting and drawing such as a border drawn around to enclose a picture, vertical and horizontal lines, crosses, radials. Talk these through with staff and parents/carers. Explain how they can indicate the presence of a schema.

5. Shape and pattern

Being involved in children's exploration of shape and pattern.

(Birth to Three Matters)

Babies

Babies will unconsciously begin to appreciate the elements of art – colour, shape, pattern and design – as these elements are all around them. Think about the mobile that hangs over the cot, or in the window, the music centre lights that flash on and off, the patterns on clothes or in the home.

Babies are fascinated by spots and squares; they encourage the development of neural pathways in the brain. Pointing out patterns and encouraging babies to touch them supports this development. Recent research in the USA shows that at four months of age babies start to rely more on shape than pattern to work out if objects placed side by side are separate or a single unit. Further studies are now looking at whether babies of eight months use shape and colour/pattern to look at objects (Duke University, http://psychweb.psych.duke.edu/department/anlab/ipl/IPL_Research.htm).

Practical activities

- Use black and white as a focus. Create an area using tiles on the floor and wall, black and white cushions, soft construction blocks, spotted, striped and patterned black and white fabric and soft toys.

- Encourage posting boxes as part of the baby room resources. Have a variety so that babies can choose which they would like to do. Group them and have a space and shape opportunity session.

- Encourage soft block play introducing cubes, cones and cylinders. This gives babies opportunities to experience the property of the shapes.

- Create a circular treasure basket that contains circular objects and a square one with square objects. Observe how the babies interact with them.

- Have a 'pattern' theme for a treasure basket – collect interesting items for the babies to explore using their hands and eyes.

Toddlers

Shape and pattern can be explored in many ways other than through art/craft. It can be how a child perceives himself in space, the shape and pattern of physical movements, or it could be musical patterns or the words and phrases repeated in poems and stories. Having a pattern or routine to the structure of the day or the week helps a child to feel more secure and in control by knowing what to expect, when.

Practical activities

- Supply ribbons, wool or strips of fabric and show the children how to weave them through railings, small branches or a grid. Help the children to weave their own bodies through the climbing frame.

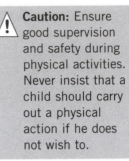

Caution: Ensure good supervision and safety during physical activities. Never insist that a child should carry out a physical action if he does not wish to.

- Read the story of 'Goldilocks and the three bears' and provide items for the role-play area such as sets of cups, plates and bowls, chairs, blankets and beds for Baby bear, Mummy bear and Daddy bear. Introduce the vocabulary 'big', 'bigger' and 'biggest'. This helps to develop mathematical language and one-to-one correspondence.

- Observe how children stack blocks and bricks and learn to overcome problems of stability. Record their efforts on a digital camera, show them the photographs and talk about the activity with them. Notice the patterns children produce during block play, matching shapes and sizes or creating symmetrical shapes.

- Mark out circles, spirals, snakes and boxes on the playground. Encourage the children to walk or ride around them. Occasionally place obstacles such as traffic cones or crates and notice the new pathways they create.

- Play circle games such as 'Ring a ring o' roses' or 'Here we go round the mulberry bush'. Encourage them to join in with the words.

- Provide coloured pegs and a strong cardboard box or washing line. Observe the way they use the pegs to make a repeating pattern. Cut strips of coloured paper into lengths and shapes and provide a pot of glue. Let the children use them freely to create patterns. They may not make a conventional pattern but talk with them about their picture and their intentions.

- Produce shape patterns on a computer using appropriate software, print their picture, and then copy using pencils or paint. Compare the pictures. Ask which they like best.

- Use a particular musical sound, such as a regular beat on a drum, to signal transition times. Help the children to make sound patterns by developing a music area. This can include wooden blocks, drums, spoons, tambourines, old clay pots. Let them explore the sounds freely. If they compose a regular pattern, show how they can follow a musical map with large, colourful symbols that tell them when it's time to beat on their drum or shake their tambourine.

Outcomes for the child

- Increased confidence and awareness
- Exploration of different media

Focus points

Being able to draw a shape or create a pattern shows real control, thought and intention rather than making random marks. Thinking through the pattern to make a bead necklace requires the ability to classify, recognise similarities and differences and make a selection of beads according to a specific attribute. These skills are the foundation of mathematical thinking.

Staff discussion

- Do you provide sets of objects and duplicate sets for the children to order, match, compare?
- Do you find time to talk with children about what they have done and show a genuine interest in their representations? Notice the colours they have used, the shapes they have made and recognise that they have had to think hard and work carefully to produce it.

6. Symbols

Discovering that one thing can stand for another.

(Birth to Three Matters)

Babies

Babies imitate real life and will often use whatever is at hand to represent something they have observed. A block of wood may represent a mobile phone; a wooden massager, one that has circular roller balls beneath it, can be wheeled along to be a car or buggy. Providing interesting natural items to allow their imaginations to work facilitates an important stage of representation.

Do not be afraid to observe and maybe be confused for a while as to the baby's logic as her representations may not be clear cut to an adult. Resist the temptation to implant ideas or correct a baby – allow her the freedom to express and imagine for herself.

Practical activities

- Collect blocks of wood, cones and misshapes. Allow free play and exploration of any of the following: tunnels and cylinders, fabric, shape and form.
- Collect vacuum cleaner hoses, hamster tubes and pipes to allow free play and the exploration of tunnels and cylinders.
- Collect samples of net curtain, voile and see-through materials to explore.
- Mix thick paint to use with small rollers and sponge rollers (available from educational suppliers). Let the babies make lines and pathways with the paint on long lengths of paper laid out on the floor.
- Allow babies to explore dough and clay – with no outcomes.
- Use simple arrow symbols to create crawl ways and pathways.
- Be aware of any important cultural symbols babies may see very early on in their home environment.

Toddlers

Toddlers begin to use shapes and symbols to stand for people and animals once they want to recreate their internal or mental images into more concrete forms, such as drawing, painting modelling and play. When engaged in pretend play they continue to use their imaginations to substitute objects for the actual or real things, for example using a brick as a car and accompanying it with a 'vroom, vroom' noise or a police siren. They enjoy pretend tea parties with imaginary drinks and food; an empty cardboard box can be a car, a rocket or a house. However, toddlers still need to have access to a stimulating environment and experiences that will enrich their understanding of life through the sensory cues of sight, sound, touch, taste and smell.

Practical activities

- Make imprints of coins, leaves and textures by covering with paper and gently rubbing with a soft crayon or pencil. Press handprints in the sand or make marks in mud or snow. Push tools into play dough or clay. This will reinforce the idea that a mark can represent an object.

- Play 'Charades' with a small group. Start by miming simple actions such as hammering, pointing to your mouth and rubbing your stomach or cupping your ear with your hand. Can the children guess what you are doing? Encourage them to have a go. Explore gestures such as thumbs up = OK, a wave = hello or goodbye, a finger on lips = shush, be quiet.

- While the children are engaged in an activity tape record their chatter and snap some digital action photographs. Later in the day play back the recording and show the photos. Talk with the children, recalling the activity, and ask them to choose some words to accompany the photos. Make some speech bubble captions to go alongside the photos using the children's comments.

- Look around the immediate environment or the local high street and collect photographs to show examples of familiar marks and signs, such as text, signs/logos, adverts. Do the children recognise any? Do they know what they mean? Try to find examples of writing from other cultures such as Chinese, Arabic, or Asian.

Outcomes for the child

- Recognising symbols and signs helps the children to make sense of their environment and find resources.

- Development of the understanding that symbols have meanings.

Focus points

A symbol is a kind of immediate shorthand that is simple yet can be used to represent a very complex idea or concept. It can be many things: an image, an object, a token, a particular colour or pattern, a gesture. For example, to an adult a cross says Christianity and a blue and white scarf can represent Chelsea Football Club. Some young children have a sophisticated understanding of advertising symbols and logos even before they are able to read. They recognise the labels on drink cans, chocolate bars, fast food outlets and TV merchandising for 'must have' toys.

Staff discussion

- Give staff some obscure items and let them consider them. Ask them to take them to their rooms and observe what children do with them – do they represent things in the same way?

- Are there zones within the setting where signs and symbols can be used to help children identify resources easily or tidy up quickly?

- Make an audit of children's personal items and note how many have been influenced by TV marketing.

References

DfES (Department for Education and Skills) (2002) *Birth to Three Matters: A Framework to Support Children in their Earliest Years.* London: DfES.

DfES (Department for Education and Skills) (2003) *Every Child Matters.* London: DfES.

DfES (Department for Education and Skills)/DWP (Department for Work and Pensions) (2003) *National Standards for Under 8s Day Care and Childminding (Full Day Care).* London: DfES.

Harpley, A. (1990) *Media Education: Bright Ideas.* London: Scholastic Publications.

3 | Being creative

Introduction

> Our task, regarding creativity, is to help children climb their own mountains, as high as possible.
>
> (Loris Malaguzzi, world famous founder and educator of the Reggio experience project, quoted in Edwards *et al.*, 1998)

The practitioner's role is central to developing children's creativity but in this area of learning the adults are not the 'ones who know', who tell the children what to do. They let the children take the lead and search alongside them, nurturing and scaffolding their ideas and interests.

Being creative can be defined as finding a new or innovative way of doing something or thinking in a different way. It is the ability to come up with fresh ideas, having an open mind and a willingness to change direction – something children are very good at doing. In this way they produce something that is individual and unique, different from anyone else's. However, in order to be creative you have to have mastered the old ways and skills and learnt the rules, a difficult process for a young child who is still in the process of learning and developing. In his book *The Human Mind* Professor Robert Winston refers to the work at Yale University of R. J. Sternberg. Sternberg suggests that young children are able to think more creatively than adults as a critical part of their brain is still being developed. Because of this they are not held back and are able to make free associations, let their imaginations fly and unself-consciously respond to sounds and experiences. Traditionally, the right side of the brain was considered the creative area but controversy continues to reign as to whether creativity is wholly right brained or if it requires elements of both sides.

Young children are not worried or even aware that their observations and creations may appear to be 'odd' to an adult. They are naturally inquisitive, curious and willing to take risks. They have a 'What if . . . ?' response when stimulated by new experiences and investigate by using all their senses, in particular the eyes, ears and hands. A baby's first emotional responses can be observed through her gestures and sounds and then later on through her pretend play, singing, dancing and representing.

There are two distinct areas that need to be combined to help a child become both competent and creative: first, he needs the opportunity to use the tools and media necessary to gain manipulative control and second, he should have the freedom to express his individuality, feelings, thoughts and emotions. In order for this to happen, the adult needs to enhance the child's exposure to positive experiences in art, music and movement and his cultural influences by providing stimulating resources and materials. Alongside the development of basic manipulative skills children need space and time to try things out, experiment, investigate, maybe make a few mistakes and try again, any time they want to. One of the essential ingredients in fostering children's creativity is for adults to value and respect a child's contribution, give constant encouragement, showing genuine interest and praise and not expecting an 'end product'.

When observing children totally involved in an experience, it is easy to recognise when they are 'in the flow'. You can identify deep concentration, enjoyment and satisfaction signifying that learning is taking place. Creativity is an essential and important part of a child's education.

1. Responding to the world

Babies quickly make sense of and respond to what they see, hear, feel, touch and smell.

(Birth to Three Matters)

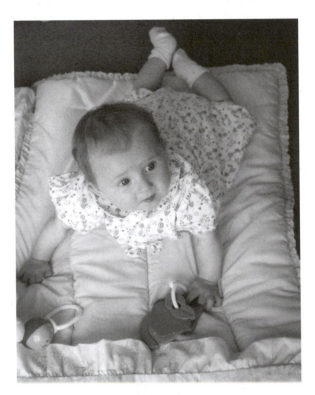

Babies

A baby explores her world mainly through her senses. Initially this exploration takes the form of 'mouthing' – so touch and tasting are the key senses used. Then as she develops her sense of sight she assimilates more – her hands and wrists strengthen and she can touch, grasp and explore. She smells her dinner, knows that her food is coming and has an emotional response – she gets excited.

The senses are a basic toolkit for babies and in order for them to be stimulated, the babies need to have real, first-hand experiences. Although at times this may be messy, it will encourage their creative responses. Experiencing the process and the raw materials are the most important part for babies – outcomes are immaterial.

Practical activities

- Provide babies with soft dough so that they can grasp and prod the material. Incorporate different aromas, colours and textures to awaken the senses. Add in some flavoured teabags to provide a gritty texture, an aroma as well as a colour. Look for teabags that have no artificial colourings. Photograph or video the babies exploring the dough and focus on their facial gestures and the sounds they make.

- Provide a space to explore colour. Use small sized parachutes or coloured fabric squares and place toys strategically on the portion of co-ordinating colour on the parachute or fabric, for example put a blue bear in the blue section. Observe how the baby responds.

- Create a collection of 'smelly' discovery bottles. Use small sports bottles that have a secure lid and put strongly smelling resources inside such as lavender or mint. Encourage the babies to squeeze the bottles and smell.

- Place cold yellow custard onto a circular kitchen tray, have another one with red jelly and a third with corn flour gloop coloured with food colouring. Encourage the babies to explore the different materials, mixing them together with their hands and watching the colours swirling and changing.

Toddlers

Creativity can arise from many different situations but in order to be creative young children have to have had real experiences. Young children still need to be able to use all their senses as they handle real materials, feeling the weight, texture and shape.

Practical activities

- Encourage free play in the water tray, making sea worlds with pebbles and shells. Add small world toys and items that float, like a miniature lilo, for imaginative sea-side play. Develop sand scenarios with rocks, twigs and toy snakes, dinosaurs or elephants. Mould damp sand into shapes and later add water to observe how wet sand behaves differently. Put some of the resources and sand onto individual food trays so that children can work independently if they wish.

- Have a wide selection of wooden blocks – some really big ones for making large-scale constructions. Plain wooden blocks allow the children to design freely as they do not restrict the imagination and can represent anything the children wish.

- Supply boxes and crates together with large pieces of fabric to create dens and secret worlds.

- Plant willow twigs. Willow grows very quickly and can be shaped to form tunnels and enclosed spaces. This will attract those children who are engaged in an enclosure or covering schema.

- Erect a tee-pee or tent to create a special quiet place for oral story-telling sessions.

- Make music outdoors. Hang a selection of metal saucepan lids from a rope and provide metal and wooden spoons and sticks to improvise percussion play.

- Set up cooking sessions using a basic muffin recipe and providing a selection of extra ingredients for the children to choose from so that they can create their own individual muffin. Include such things as dried fruit, fresh fruit and berries, orange and lemon peel.

> ⚠️ **Caution:** Be wary about including any nuts in cooking sessions. Check food allergies with parents/carers.

Outcomes for the child

- Children have the freedom to explore their own imagination.
- Confidence.
- Curiosity based on the use of their senses.
- Movement and sounds are linked in a cognitive way.
- An ability to understand and make sense of their experiences.

Focus points

Many toys for children are made from 70 per cent PVC that includes vinyl chloride, a known carcinogen and some also have additives such as lead and cadmium. In addition, they are not biodegradable. When purchasing plastic toys look for the safer option, labelled #1 or #2, as these are easier to recycle and do not produce so many toxins. Avoid those labelled PVC or #3.

Simple toys made from natural materials are more open ended and allow children to use them in a variety of ways. Many of the commercially marketed toys and dressing-up clothes only allow them to be used in a restricted way. A plastic cooker is a cooker yet a plain cardboard box can be a rocket, a bus or a den. A printed superhero suit dictates what you have to be, but with a cloak or a length of silk material you can free your imagination and become anyone or anything you wish. If a wooden toy breaks, it can be repaired or glued but a plastic toy remains broken.

Staff discussion

- Observe how children use the toys. Do they play with them the way the manufacturer designed them to be used or do the children adapt them to suit the moment?
- Audit your resources and throw out any that are broken or have missing parts. Presenting resources in an attractive or novel way can stimulate and inspire the children to engage with them. Add unusual items to renew interest – for example, introduce different sizes and shapes of ramps for toy vehicles to be 'driven' down, put tubes, pipes, sieves, or bubbles in the water tray.

2. Recognising schemas

Encourage independence as young children explore particular patterns of thought or movement, sometimes referred to as Schemas.
(Birth to Three Matters)

Babies

There is more evidence available that supports toddlers' schematic behaviour than for babies; however, some babies do exhibit particular schemas quite clearly and have been tracked from babyhood through to infanthood. For example, babies can be observed making repeated vertical and horizontal marks in split milk or food and later choose to do this with crayons or in sand. A schema is defined by Chris Athey (1990) as 'A pattern of repeatable behaviour into which experiences are assimilated and that are gradually coordinated'. Athey names schemas according to their characteristics such as vertical or horizontal, transportation, radial, enveloping. The *Birth to Three Matters* guidelines (DfES, 2002) provide further information on the accompanying CD which assists practitioners who have had little experience or have not researched this fascinating subject. If practitioners observe babies carefully, they may see some early signs of schemas as some of their babies begin to show repeated behaviour patterns.

Practical activities

- Choose collections for treasure baskets that are centred on a child's schematic behaviour. For example, if a child encloses or covers items (enclosure schema) provide small world play items, such as dolls, animals or Mobilo, and samples of cloths, squares of material, scarves and boxes to support his interest.

- A transporting schema is evident when babies repeatedly move toys from one place to another in quite a systematic way. Provide a collection of different containers, boxes, baskets and bags to facilitate this and of course the items to transport such as bricks or balls.

- A rotational schema involves circular movements and rolling. Use sleep mats or exercise mats to encourage rolling and turning. Have toys that twist and turn such as cogs and wheels.

Toddlers

Young children learn by watching, listening, exploring then they represent their experiences by doing. This is what adults call play and it is what makes learning fun. What children want to learn is often driven by their schema and identified by a consuming interest in a particular concept, recognisable by a repeating pattern of behaviour. Schemas are frequently mathematically based and provide the foundation for future understanding of abstract concepts. Once an adult tunes in to 'schema watching' she can identify the child's current interest. What appears to be a child flitting randomly from one activity to another is in fact his pursuit of his schema. For example, a child may go from being hidden underneath a parachute to putting objects into a saucepan and covering them with lids and then move on to covering his hands with paint. All these activities are interwoven and have the common schema of covering or enveloping. Young children need to be given the opportunity and freedom to pursue their schema until the inner drive has been satisfied.

Practical activities

Actual activities will depend on the children's current schemas. However, helping children to help themselves so that they become independent and autonomous will allow them to follow their schema and also develop their self-confidence and belief in their own ability.

- Enable young children to do things for themselves such as pouring their own juice. Help them to put on their aprons by attaching simple Velcro fastenings. Celebrate when they achieve stages of personal independence with genuine praise especially in the areas of toileting, feeding and self-discipline. Ensure it's not empty praise but real and genuine.

- Make sure that the setting has simple, clear rules, known boundaries and expectations of behaviour – for example, when and where the bikes are used, how many children can safely play on the climbing frame, why children do not go out of the gate.

- Help children to know where resources are kept, how to use them and return them easily. Have see-through containers or photographs of the contents that are easily accessible and at child height. Supply child-sized brush and dustpans, cloths and rubbish bin and praise them when they tidy up or clean up their own spills.

- Stock the creative zone with multi-sensory resources, a wide range of materials, tools for mark making, cutting and joining. In order to make an informed choice children have to have had previous experience of the materials. Therefore, they need time to get to know the resources. To stimulate their interest and exploratory drive introduce new, unfamiliar items.

Outcomes for the child

- Development of self-confidence and self-belief.
- Self-satisfaction at being able to work through a schema if it is supported.
- Immersion in a cognitive need.
- Having a unique need met.

Focus points

It can be that everything in the child's daily activities has been planned for by the adult, who may have her own agenda or targets, but this does not take into account the young child's current interests and needs. By facilitating child-initiated activities, the practitioner is empowering the children to become responsible for their own learning and needs. Through talk and reflection, adults can support children by helping them to plan what they want to do and provide them with the necessary resources. In 1978, Lev Vygotsky promoted the idea of the 'the zone of proximal development'. He suggests that what the child could manage now (can nearly do) with a little bit of help he would soon be able to achieve independently. This has become known as 'scaffolding'.

Staff discussion

- Observe, talk, and listen to what children are trying to do. Assess how much they could achieve with a little more help from an adult. Record your observations, possible action and lines of enquiry.
- Plan time in the day to reflect with the children and talk about what they have done and what they would like to do. Note what they say.

- Review how you help children to develop responsibility and become independent. Are you always consistent in your approach and responses?
- Explore the research on schemas. Check out any or all of the following:

    Chris Athey, *Extending Thought in Young Children* (Paul Chapman Publishing, 1990)

    Tina Bruce, *Time to Play in Early Childhood Education* (Hodder and Stoughton, 1991)

    Jerome Bruner and Helen Haste, *Making Sense* (Routledge, 1987)

    Cathy Nutbrown, *Threads of Thinking* (Paul Chapman Publishing, 1994)

    Margy Whalley, *Learning to be Strong* (Hodder and Stoughton, 1994)

3. Experimenting

Observe the movements and sounds babies make . . . [a]s children become more skilful in using language and other forms of communication, such as dance, music . . .

(*Birth to Three Matters*)

Babies

Babies like to observe moving objects whether it's the mobile over their cot or their own hands and feet. When they get excited about a new toy or seeing a new face, they show their emotions through the movement of their bodies – wriggling, stretching and rearing up. Once their vocal sounds are developed, they use their cries to signal their immediate needs. Key persons and parents soon identify these sounds, understand and respond thereby reinforcing the babies' signals.

Babies can be actively creative as they explore paint, enjoying the movement of their bodies, the sensation of the paint and the process. Babies are like impressionist artists in that the creative outcome does not have to represent anything specific, although often parents expect to see an end product.

Dancing and moving in an uninhibited way often occurs in early childhood but is lost as children get older and become self-conscious. Babies and toddlers should be able to enjoy this wonderful period and adults should support, enable and encourage this creative form of expression.

Practical activities

- Lay an exercise mat or several sleep mats along the floor in a pathway. Place a trail of sounds along them, for example small bells, shakers, rattles or unused squeaky toys. Put these into small transparent containers and encourage the baby to crawl along the pathway, lift out the objects, explore them and discover the sounds.

- Place items that make different sounds in a play tunnel, equally spaced from the entrance, middle and end. Show where the items are and what they sound like. This will encourage the babies to move through the tunnel and explore the objects. Listen for the babies' responses and watch their gestures and behaviour.

- Play some rhythmic music to encourage the babies to move, sway or rock. Hold young babies safely and securely, sharing the experience with them. Have fun.

- Use music that has a limited range such as African or Indonesian Gamelan music that features mainly gongs and percussion instruments and uses just a few notes. Provide spoons and saucepans for the babies to bang on and join in as an accompaniment.

- Babies hear the music of the day and pick up on catchy tunes (such as The Crazy Frog Song). Talk with parents/carers about the kind of music they like to hear at home and offer it in your setting.

- Provide a collection of discovery bottles – call it your natural collection. Use the very small sized water bottles. Place some natural items inside, such as lentils, peas, gravel, rice and pasta. Secure the tops well. Encourage the children to shake them and roll them while listening to music.

Toddlers

Dance and music are closely linked as our sense of hearing (the auditory nerve) connects with all the muscles in the body. Sound vibrations within our ears affect our sense of balance which is essential for the control of movement. Games that involve sound, touch and movement are important for growth and development.

Skills such as listening to sounds and being able to discriminate between them and remember them, together with rhythm and pattern, are the foundations for learning language.

Practical activities

- Provide a wide range of objects for the children to explore freely and combine in their own way to make sounds, patterns and rhythms. Look for large and small shells, bottle tops and buttons threaded to make shakers, bubble wrap and scrunched-up paper, sand paper blocks, wood blocks, terracotta pots, metal kitchen utensils. Attach objects to metal coat hangers so that they can be suspended and then struck with a metal spoon. Notice if the children compose a repeating pattern. When outside explore the sound made by clinking along a metal fence.

  > **Caution:** Supervise carefully small items that could be swallowed.

- Encourage the children to discover the many different sounds they can make with their own bodies, such as toe tapping, finger clicking, hand clapping. Then focus on the mouth, lips, tongue and teeth. Challenge them to change the intensity of the sounds from loud to very quiet and the speed from slow to fast. Read *Who's Making That Noise?* by Philip Hawthorn and Jenny Tyler (Usborne, 2004).

- Let the children choose the music to dance to. Observe the natural movements they employ, for example sliding, crawling, stamping and twirling. Encourage wide open arm movements by providing ribbons and scarves. Play 'Follow my leader', clapping to a steady beat and establishing a pattern. Introduce bubbles and balloons to catch or follow. Explore creating different body shapes – wide legs, curled up, jumping jack and so forth. Play the DVD/video 'Angelina Ballerina' (see Resources).

- Play a version of 'Blind man's bluff' where the children listen carefully and identify what the sounds are and where they are located. Start with easily identifiable sounds such as a door slamming, click clack of high heels and then progress to listening for quieter background sounds such as a tap dripping. Ask the children if they can remember the first sound they hear when they wake up in the morning. Talk about sounds that are signals or warnings: a mobile phone, door bell, fire alarm, police siren.

- Make a tape (ideally with the children) of everyday sounds – a vacuum cleaner, microwave, the post dropping through a letter box, etc. – similar to the one above but different.

Outcomes for the child

- Learning to maintain a steady beat develops hand–eye control.
- Being able to discriminate between sounds helps the development of language.
- Clapping integrates the left- and right-hand sides of the brain.

Focus points

Music is an essential part of our daily lives and is included in important events such as social gatherings, celebrations, festivals and family life. It is a vital part of some cultures. Young children are attracted to sounds and rhythms as they echo the rhythms of the body, the heartbeat and pulse. Banging on a drum or stamping feet can help a lively toddler let off steam or coax and distract one from unwanted behaviour. On the other hand, soft, melodic tunes can create a calm and relaxed atmosphere. Making up songs about daily activities can help to get the job done faster, for example 'This is the way we fasten our coat'.

Staff discussion

- Explore the possibilities of a trip to the ballet or a musical. Invite dancers and musicians to the setting.
- Collect a range of dance and music videos from all around the world so that the children are exposed to a wide variety of creative forms.
- Review your resources to include tape recorders, CD players and electronic keyboards. Ensure you have a wide variety of music from around the world. Invest in simple musical instruments such as xylophones, bells, drums and tambourines.

4. Competence

For young children the process of creating is more important than an end product.

(*Birth to Three Matters*)

Babies

Babies use their senses to experience colour, shape and form. Before they begin to make representations or recognisable (to adults) end products they need to immerse themselves in the process part of the learning experience. Capturing their experiences through photographs or video is an essential part of appreciating the importance of 'the process' as their facial expressions and body language are key indicators. Often the resources, for example paint or gloop, totally absorb the babies' attention and this deep involvement is a sign of one of the early stages of learning. The process combines the engagement with the resources as well as the physical activity that occurs with those resources.

Practical activities

- Immerse a baby in colour. Choose, for example, yellow and then collect voile, ballerina netting, yellow materials, yellow sheets. Cover some sleep mats or exercise mats in the chosen colour and then set out all the yellow materials, adding yellow toys or items. Allow the baby to lie on them, crawl over them or just experience the power of one colour in one place.

- Collect lots of leaves and put them in a ball pool or paddling pool and allow a seated baby to explore them. Later place them on a table or high chair surface and encourage them to pat and stick them onto a surface. Looking and holding the leaves and patting are the most important things – this is the process; the paper product may be tatty and disorganised but this does not matter.

- Collect all kinds of card and shiny paper and encourage babies to explore them, scrunch them and twist or wave them in the air.

- Cover balls in paint and let babies roll them over large sheets of paper. Inevitably, there will be handprints and smudges but this is representing the process. Photographing the event will record some of the learning and facial gestures which can show emotions such as pleasure, confusion and delight.

Toddlers

When young children are totally involved in an activity, the learning potential is increased and they have a heightened sense of satisfaction in their own achievements. Most young children are curious and naturally inquisitive, keen to explore new situations and experiences. Child-initiated activities, rather than those directed by the adult, allow the children to use their imagination and ingenuity. For example, a piece of silk fabric can be a cloak, a river or a cloud; a strong cardboard box has endless possibilities – you can climb into it and pretend it's a car going to visit a friend and then suddenly it becomes the friend's house. The actual process of being creative is more important than having a product.

Practical activities

- Set up an investigation resource of shiny materials, for example a stainless steel teapot, large serving spoons, car wheel hubs, non-breakable Christmas decorations and foil. Allow the children free play with the items so they can explore their reflections. Provide flexible acrylic mirror tiles which bend to create both concave and convex images. The children enjoy seeing their faces and bodies distorted, lengthened and widened like in a fun house. Add a selection of magnifying mirrors and kaleidoscopes.

- Have a selection of coloured transparencies and manipulate them on a light box or overhead projector. Let the children explore how colours intensify and shapes change when they are placed on top of each other. Experiment with different objects, small toys, leaves and include some shapes/items that are not transparent.

- Let the children dance freely, inside and outside, to a wide range of music. Provide silk scarves or wrist bracelets made from small bells, buttons or shells.

Be aware that the music may dictate how the children respond; it can reflect their mood and emotions, calm or excite them. Encourage them to listen to music while they are engaged in creative activities and notice if it has an effect on their behaviour, their mood or concentration.

- Toddlers live in the moment, the now. Provide experiences that are just for fun or that delight the senses – bubbles, corn flour 'gloop', shaving foam, water and ice. Change the colours with vegetable dyes and freeze water into animal shapes to provide a different stimulation.

- Organise visits to local markets, flower shops, parks and nature where children can experience first hand the variety of colours, shapes, noises and smells.

Outcomes for the child

- Children gain confidence in their own abilities.
- Developing skills as they experiment.
- Expressing ideas, feelings and emotions.
- Becoming involved which leads to concentration and persistence.

Focus points

Adults support children's creativity by helping to set their imaginations in motion, providing the space, time and materials and, if required, direction and help. Children need to be able to develop their own capabilities, make decisions and express themselves in ways that reflect their individual imagination.

Staff discussion

- Review how and why you use the following: templates, stencils and step-by-step 'follow me' processes. Are activities used to impose adult ideas and perceptions of what things should look like and how things should be?

- Ask who benefits from the products produced by children. Is it that the setting gets to display their work, parents have something tangible or for the satisfaction and experience of the child?

- Explore the possibilities of getting local artists, dancers and musicians to visit the setting and work with the children.

- Resources: flexible acrylic tiles can be obtained from craft suppliers or a number of outlets on the internet.

5. Being resourceful

Creative activity provides opportunities to be resourceful in finding different ways of doing and making things.

(Birth to Three Matters)

Babies

Babies and toddlers explore the world using all their senses and in time begin to build up an understanding and form relationships between objects and materials. Their explorations can be very involved and at times almost intense. Babies need to have open-ended opportunities and time to immerse themselves in their activity. Creativity needs freedom to thrive. Often a well-meaning adult leads them or instructs them. Simple collection of items that have similarities or are quite different, presented in an inviting way, encourages choice and autonomy. Babies just enjoy the exploration, although some will investigate with caution, and then later as they build up their confidence they will use them in their own individual way.

Practical activities

- Explore a collection of paper-based materials with a variety of textures, sounds and colours. Present these attractively on a mat on the floor or in a treasure basket.

- Empty a paddling pool or activity pool and fill it with woven balls, soft balls, fruit, such as oranges and grapefruit, so babies can explore heavy and light, soft and hard, different colours and textures.

- Purchase a bubble maker machine (available in Early Learning stores and larger toy shops) and put music on in the background, sit the baby on the floor and start the machine up. Watch the wonder and fun on the baby's face.

- Make a lilac zone – this is a very calming colour. Hang materials from the ceiling; co-ordinate with lilac cushions and lilac-coloured soft toys to cuddle. Play soft, calming music and create mobiles using lilac feathers. Allow the babies to enjoy this quiet, calm space as they get tired or just need a calm place where they start or end the day.

Toddlers

Toddlers need to have experienced a wide variety of materials and situations before they can make an informed and independent decision and be creative in their own unique way. They can change their way of doing or thinking and look at things from a new and different viewpoint. Initially they learn through their senses and by repetition and practice – for example, when constructing and building they enjoy knocking things down and building them up again, perhaps with slight changes and improvements.

Practical activities

- Cover a table with newspaper and provide a wide variety of materials for joining and gluing. Include items such as: sticky tape, a stapler, string, scissors, bank tags, hole punch. Add a variety of found resources (junk), cardboard boxes, feathers, shells, wood shavings, wrapping paper, magazines and catalogues, seeds, yogurt pots, straws, felt tip pens and so on – the list is endless.

Caution: Supervise the use of small items that may be put in the mouth. Demonstrate the way to use tools. Let the children cut, tear, and glue and create pictures, models and collages.

- Develop the above activity by controlling the selection of materials so that the children create using specific textures, patterns or colours.

- Provide thick and creamy paint and let the children enjoy building up colours. Vary the activity by adding extra texture to the paint, for example paste, oats, seeds, sand and sparkles.

- Collect unwanted photographs and cut them up to make new picture collages.

- Introduce different or unusual items into small world play and observe how the children use them, for example a garlic press, old clockwork parts, and a collection of small boxes or containers.

- Provide materials so that the children can design their own worlds in the sand or water tray using stones, shells, pebbles, different colours and sizes of gravel. Introduce chutes and ramps made from plumbers' pipes, guttering and transparent hoses.

- Support the children with materials for them to create their own dens, inside or outside – for example, plastic milk crates, large wooden blocks, a strong and stable clothes airer covered with light fabric.

Outcomes for the child

- Increased confidence and self-expression.
- Development of muscles in the hands and fingers giving improved manipulative skills.
- Increased knowledge through experimenting in joining and fixing materials together.
- Satisfaction and enjoyment of making their own unique models based on their mental images.

Focus points

Many of the early childhood resources are made from plastic. It is an environmentally expensive and wasteful resource and in addition, the designs of some items limit the way they can be used. A plastic cooker is always just that whereas a plain wooden block can become anything in a child's imagination. By providing real props and natural resources, the children learn the properties of materials and develop mathematical concepts of weight, height, size, volume and texture. Through working with plain wooden blocks, they learn about shape and size, balance and symmetry. They enjoy simple activities such as collecting, tearing, and pasting, sorting and looking at materials and many of these activities are inexpensive options yet provide valuable learning opportunities.

Staff discussion

- Explore the possibility of sourcing good quality scrap materials. Some towns have designated scrap stores that settings can use. Encourage parents to collect boxes, bottles and transparent containers. A large, strong cardboard box, such as those used to pack TVs or washing machines, can provide endless opportunities for imaginative play.

- Demonstrate how to use tools such as scissors, staplers and sticky tape correctly. Have these tools readily available and accessible in a central area.

- Aim to give the children ample time to explore, experiment and create at their own pace.

- Use unstructured sessions as a valuable time to observe and note the children's developing skills and capabilities.

6. Meeting diverse needs

The materials offered should reflect a wide variety of cultural settings and allow children to experience many forms of creative expression.

(*Birth to Three Matters*)

Babies

From the moment of birth, babies experience the cultural ethos that surrounds them. The smell of their foods, the look and colour of their family's clothes, the way they dress their hair and the rituals that link to their culture. These are familiar early experiences but when they socialise with others in a setting outside their home they begin to see that others are not always the same. Having a diverse group of cultures provides a setting with breadth and depth. It potentially opens up a rich bank of resources and opportunities. Encouraging diversity requires staff to have an openness of mind and respect in order to take on board knowledge and understanding and be a true facilitator of every child's unique needs.

Practical activities

- Create a treasure basket which displays a variety of cultural items such as Indonesian spoons, balti dishes or artefacts from the Far East and Eastern Europe. Ask parents to assist by providing items made of natural materials and those that show aspects of their culture.

- Collect lengths of cloth with bright and vibrant designs such as saris or African patterned material. Allow free exploration of these.

- Provide a variety of fruit and vegetables for the babies to explore the texture, shape and smell, and if appropriate, to taste.

- Use small scarves, saris or short lengths of fabric (with a variety of traditional patterns on) to use for 'parachute' play. Add a small soft ball for babies to try and roll backwards and forwards along the cloth or to lift up and drop.

- Make a collection of world music on CD. Play this each day on arrival to greet the babies and their families.

Toddlers

Young children are growing up in a diverse and multicultural environment that offers rich opportunities to try a range of different experiences. Through this subtle permeation of cultures, they can explore aspects of creativity that range from clay, through music to cookery and gardening.

Practical activities

- Visit the local environment for opportunities that show different ways of life, such as products displayed in shops and their packaging, signs in different scripts, music, fast food, hairdressers, etc. Use the information to create an imaginative play area that reflects the realities of the children's daily lives. This can deepen and extend the children's sense of identity and pride in their family culture.

- Talk with parents to gain an insight into the children's lives and interests. Do they enjoy fishing with Dad? Does the family visit relatives or take care of older parents at home? Are there any special activities that the family does together? Value the information and use it to recreate activities for the children. For example, a child whose family likes to go camping will feel confident and keen to share his experiences if you erect a tent in the imaginative play area.

- Talk with the children and find out what they watch on TV, who are their favourite characters, books, toys and games? Provide resources that link these interests with activities in the setting. The children will recreate adventures they have watched on TV or video – for example, have 'Bob the builder' in the sand tray with diggers and lorries, or 'Nemo' in the water tray. Look for matching software programs for the computer.

- Expand the range of music and songs available for the children to self-select to incorporate those that reflect their family's birth countries and culture.

- Display pictures of African or Aboriginal paintings. Many tell a visual story or a journey. These are closely linked to a dab schema and may inspire children to create their own versions.

- Look for ways to incorporate traditional social events such as weddings in the setting. Encourage parents to share their wedding photographs and talk about the ceremonies and if you are lucky they may bring in traditional bridal gowns. Develop the wedding theme in the imaginative play area with photos, decorations, dressing up and food.

- Provide a range of books in dual languages. Show the children how each script is read – some left to right, others right to left, etc. (see Resources).

Outcomes for the child

- Development of a positive sense of identity.
- Understanding and acknowledging that people have similarities and differences.
- Children gain respect for other cultures and value their own.

Focus points

It is not possible to 'grow' people unless you nurture their roots.

(Martin Luther King, Jr)

One of a practitioner's skills is to help children feel secure when they make the transition from home to a setting. Valuing their family background, beliefs and customs while focusing on their strengths will be a major part of this.

Staff discussion

- Develop your own awareness of world music – invite parents to come in and play their own cultural instruments.

- Explore ways in which the adults in the setting can learn new experiences, skills or techniques such as drumming, dancing or working alongside an artist.

- Look in arts centres for a directory of potters, sculptures, wood carvers.

- Have a cookery collection that reflects the diverse nature of your community.

- Ensure that in the book area there are dual language books and that staff are aware of the culture and language that they reflect.

- Think across all areas of the setting – do you use multicultural play dough? Do you provide a range of paints, crayons, paper that can reflect skin colour?

- Examine aspects of the local environment for a diversity of art, pattern, design and artistic skills.

- When going for walks or visits out, are these taking in all aspects of diversity?

⚠ **Caution:** Be aware that all adults who come to work with the children require a CRB (Criminal Records Bureau) disclosure. Do not leave them unsupervised with the children.

References

Athey, C. (1990) *Extending Thought in Young Children*. London: Paul Chapman Publishing.

Bruce, T. (1991) *Time to Play in Early Childhood Education*. London: Hodder and Stoughton.

Bruner, J. S. and Haste, H. (1987) *Making Sense*. London: Routledge.

Csikzentmihaly, M. (1996) *Creativity*. New York: HarperCollins.

DfES (Department for Education and Skills) (2002) *Birth to Three Matters: A Framework to Support Children in their Earliest Years*. London: DfES.

DfES (Department for Education and Skills) (2003) *Every Child Matters*. London: DfES.

DfES (Department for Education and Skills)/DWP (Department for Work and Pensions) (2003) *National Standards for Under 8s Day Care and Childminding (Full Day Care)*. London: DfES.

Edwards, C., Gandini, L. and Foreman, G. (eds) (1998) *The Hundred Languages of Children: The Reggio Emilia Approach – Advanced Reflections,* second edition. London: Ablex Publishing Corporation.

Harpley, A. (2003) *More Play Sense*. London: National Association of Toy and Leisure Libraries.

Hawthorne, P. and Tyler, J. (2004) *Who's Making That Noise?* London: Usborne.

Nutbrown, C. (1994) *Threads of Thinking*. London: Paul Chapman Publishing.

Whalley, M. (1994) *Learning to be Strong: Setting Up a Neighbourhood Service for Under-Fives and Their Families*. London: Hodder and Stoughton.

Winston, R. (2004) *The Human Mind: And How to Make the Most of It*. London: Bantam.

Resources

A wide variety of DVDs, books and merchandise on Angelina Ballerina is available at www.angelinaballerina.com

A selection of dual language books can be found at Mantra Lingua Publishers (www.mantralingua.com) and Milet Publishers (www.milet.com).

Note

Article 31 of the United Nations Convention on the Rights of the Child (1989), adopted in the UK in 1996, reads as follows:

> Every child has the right to rest and leisure, to engage in play and recreational activities appropriate to the age of the child and to participate freely in cultural life and the arts.

Being imaginative

Introduction

Young children have the ability to enter an imaginary world where they can reduce complex ideas into something that, for them, has understandable dimensions – a place where they can try out their thoughts and emotions. They have an inner drive, a compulsion to explore and experiment to find out about their life and how things work. They will often repeat experiences until they are satisfied.

'Let's pretend we can fly!'. Why imaginative play?

Pretend play is an important part of growing up and has long-term benefits. Many activities involve using both hemispheres of the brain in a balanced way, cognitive functioning is developed and learning ability increases. Play becomes a rehearsal for the future. It can be seen that when playing, children concentrate and become highly involved in the activity. Through pretend play, they can express their concerns and their feelings while they clarify fuzzy thinking in a safe environment – one that they organise and control. If a situation gets too hard, they can stop, change direction and start again. During imaginative play, they use all the information they have gleaned from their world and family life: adults' behaviour and values, stories, conversations and TV. Sometimes events will change as they add their own interpretation or flights of fancy and as their play script evolves. Imaginative play allows a young child to try out what it feels like to be someone else, take on a different character, and feel the urgency of a fireman or the concern of the doctor. It can be a chance to express his fears.

Unfortunately, the current trend for young children to be pressurised into becoming literate and numerate as early as possible may reduce the time that practitioners feel can be usefully spent on play. If practitioners are overly concerned about accountability, they may question the purpose of free or spontaneous play. They might even feel the need to jump in and intervene, directing the play towards a more structured activity. There are times when adult-directed play has an important place within the early years programme; it can be a vehicle for learning and providing the tools and the stimulus. Yet the time a child spends in imaginative play is when the brain has a chance to assimilate new learning and process it through full mind/body integration. If children have not had positive opportunities for this to happen, they could find understanding abstract concepts difficult, feel frustrated and be put off learning for life.

Observing children engaged in imaginative play provides an ideal opportunity for adults to assess their development. Young children naturally demonstrate what they have understood, where they are at, what interests them and what their fears and anxieties are. A useful assessment tool is to capture the significant moments of the play on video or a digital camera. This can be used to promote a valuable discussion with colleagues or parents/carers that helps to give an insight into 'what makes them tick' and what future action is needed. Play follows a developmental pattern that begins with an exploratory drive, then moves into a constructive phase, which is followed by dramatic play and later play that has clear rules and limits. During imaginative play children make choices, build up their self-esteem and confidence. The practitioners' role is to provide the time, the space, the resources and encouragement. Educationalist Janet Moyles (1989) has likened play to 'a pebble on a pond': 'the ripples from the exploratory play... allow a spiral of learning spreading ever outwards'.

1. Spaces and opportunities

Create spaces and opportunities for quiet and noisy play providing opportunities for adults and children to act as playmates, observers, initiators.

(*Birth to Three Matters*)

Babies

From birth, babies begin the process of understanding their world – from being in a small space, the womb, to being born. During the first few months, they spend their time sleeping, feeding and being held. Very young babies are startled by sudden changes in sounds or the arrival of a new face; they often show distress when a stranger enters their safe place!

It is important in day care to have a quiet area with appropriate seating where an adult can hold a young baby or a comfortable area with support cushions. Bean bags are not really appropriate for this young age group as suffocation is a real risk – the small materials in a bean bag mould around the body shape quickly. Babies do get very excited though and once they find their voice they enjoy activities that stimulate them such as watching bubbles and listening to music. Babies also enjoy messy play such as painting. Sometimes the practitioner might want to organise 'noisy areas'; however, this spontaneous play means noise builds up as the baby enjoys and gets involved with the adult.

Practical activities

- Make a quiet zone in a baby room – think about muted colours, soft furnishings, floor coverings, small wicker baskets of books and hand-muted wind chimes that produce relaxing sounds. Play soft music – a kind of 'chill out' zone for babies!

- Use carpets and mats to make a zone. Have an area with rattles all displayed in a low lipped container so the babies can self-select – this would be a 'shake, rattle and roll' zone.

- Hang ribbons, streamers or balloons down from the ceiling to make an area where you can gather to sing songs.

- Use pop-up tents or an empty ball pool to create an area for babies to experience activities such as exploring interesting materials or looking at books or photograph albums.

- Using safe mirror tiles to cover the lower half of a wall and the adjacent floor area. This denotes an area where pictures of faces can be displayed and where babies can see their own reflections and faces.

Toddlers

Toddlers can often be full of contradictions and change like the wind: one minute they are purposeful and decisive and then a few moments later they're looking for the comfort of a favourite toy and the security of familiar routines. Like whirlwinds they display full force energy yet tire quickly and easily. As they learn to socialise and play co-operatively with others, it can become intense, noisy, and even stormy. The pretend play area may need to have flexible boundaries as the action can often move from place to place as new locations are identified to facilitate the needs of the play. Resources can be simple as the children's imaginations will improvise, adapt and invent so that the ordinary can become magical. Having access to an outdoor space is important, where the children have the freedom to run and shout without inhibitions.

Practical activities

- Provide a safe area where the children can enjoy a 'rough and tumble'. Use large floor cushions, foam squares, tunnels or purchase soft play equipment.

> **Caution:** Supervise carefully. Have clear rules about safety and numbers that can play at any one time.

- Tell the story *We're Going on a Bear Hunt* by Michael Rosen. Create areas outside using simple resources to designate the different scary areas described in the story: a camouflage net for the dark forest; some textured or coloured tiles for the 'oozy mud'; and blankets to form a dark cave. Be prepared with some calming-down strategies if the play gets too vigorous.

- Once the children have gained confidence and skill with wheeled toys, introduce new stimulus and challenges. Mark off 'parking areas' or garages where the children can learn to manoeuvre into spaces. Create a pathway with traffic cones to steer around. Use a bucket of water and sponges to create a 'car wash'.

- Provide gravel, pebbles and small boxes for the children to use to fill up dumper trucks and lorries and engage in transporting play. Fit beepers, bells or horns so that they can make the appropriate noises. Use simple walkie-talkies for the transport drivers to communicate to base.

- Collect strong, large cardboard boxes and observe how the children use them. Do they jump in and out, bash them down, climb inside or make them into houses, boats or rocket ships? Do they want to add on any decorations, marks, paint?

- Take a small group for a visit to a local amenity such as the Post Office, a corner shop or supermarket. Follow up by creating a role-play area equipped with suitable resources. For example, a Post Office needs a counter, forms, stamps, letters and parcels, sorting boxes, telephones and a till. Join in the play and model the behaviour, weighing parcels, giving out forms and making conversation, asking questions. Then quietly leave the children to continue. Intervene when the play seems to be 'stuck' or needs to change direction. Introduce a new item such as a piece of technology. Read the story of *The Jolly Postman, or Other People's Letters* by Allan and Janet Ahlberg.

- Hide a broken toy outside and then help the children to 'discover' it and rescue it. Provide items so that they can care for the toy: bandages, plasters, etc. Let the children create a cosy bedroom and make special food. Ask 'How can we find out who it belongs to?' Talk about how they would feel if they lost their favourite toy.

Outcomes for the child

- Exploring personal spaces and feeling comfortable.
- Learning to share personal physical space and making contact with others in an area.
- Developing social skills, sharing and co-operating.
- Linking thoughts with action.
- Exploring roles and other points of view.

Focus points

Young children appear to have fewer chances to enjoy the freedom of outdoor play and this may be due to child protection fears or parents'/carers' work constraints. Many children's 'play' is experienced through structured after-school programmes, holiday play schemes or commercial play centres. An important aspect of growing up and preparing for later life is learning to be aware of risks and how to asses them.

Staff discussion

- Adults need to show the children that they value imaginative play just as much as any of the activities planned for or directed by the adult. How can they do this?
- Observe and identify any developing skills that are visible during imaginative play. What is the level of the children's involvement and concentration? Capture on video or digital camera to construct a learning journey. Discuss with colleagues how to support and extend the learning.
- Take a step back and assess how well the available space caters for children's imaginative play, both indoors and outside. Is it organised for the benefit and ease of adults or for the children? Can the smallest child reach and access resources easily and safely? Is the role-play area attractive, inviting and uncluttered? Are their areas for quiet reflection as well as vigorous play?

2. Imitating

Young babies enjoy learning by imitating others.

(*Birth to Three Matters*)

Babies

Babies observe others closely and if practitioners make similar sounds to a baby, she begins a communication game, testing out and repeating, waiting to mirror a new response. The learning process is one of imitation and repetition. Babies watch other babies and begin a dialogue without words, using gestures, body language and sound. The benefits of imitation should not be underestimated.

Imitation also brings the feeling of knowing that something has been done and it is OK. A confident baby may use this experience as a signal that she can continue, and if this new step is greeted with 'Oh, you are clever. Good boy/girl', said in a warm tone, then well-being and a disposition to learn begins to be created.

Practical activities

- Have large black and white photographs to give babies visual clues. For example, if a baby is waving in the photograph, then the practitioner can use this, point and say 'Wave bye bye' to baby.

- Imitation is fostered by using large low level mirrors with pull up bars positioned in front of them.

- Imitation of sounds can be developed by using a good range of books that have in-built sounds in them.

- Make a sound basket so that it can be used as a stimulus for copying sounds.

- Swaying to music is soon picked up by babies. They will imitate an adult or another child as they join in with the musical rhythms or beat.

- An adult tapping and banging a spoon on a hard surface encourages a follow-up imitation.

- Remember to use tactile experiences to encourage imitation like rubbing noses, nodding your head, blowing a kiss. Babies soon pick up such signals.

Toddlers

During imaginative play, young children practise skills they will need later in life. Many of these they learn by copying the behaviour and conversations of the significant adults in their everyday life. By recreating their familiar world at their own level of understanding, they can try to make sense of it within a safe environment – one that is under their control. In this way, they learn to socialise, solve problems, acquire skills and learn how to use and apply them. It does not matter if they don't get it right first time; if they make mistakes, they can change direction and change the scenario of the play.

Practical activities

- Young children want to explore their daily life and home play. Set up a role-play area with family related themes. Equip it with child-sized tools that replicate life at home. Make up stories about simple everyday happenings and personalise them by using the child's own name as the central character.

- Collect telephones, old mobile phones or toy telephones that ring. Interact with the children and encourage them to use specific telephone language such as 'Hello, who is calling? Can I help you?'

- Take note of the children's news. Important events such as going to a wedding, the birth of a baby sister or brother, a visit to Disney World can be the basis for role play and will enable the children to remember, recall and relive their experiences.

- Create a picnic basket with a cloth, cushions, plates, cups and 'food'. Sit with the children and a selection of soft toys. Role play eating, drinking and feeding the toys. Read stories such as Richard Scarry's *Please and Thank You Book* or Judith Kerr's *The Tiger Who Came to Tea* that help children to learn to share and be polite.

Outcomes for the child

- The feeling of being part of a dialogue or game – belonging.
- Being acknowledged.
- Being interdependent.
- Building up knowledge and understanding of their familiar world.
- Looking for ways to solve problems.

Focus points

Young children don't always need to have the real objects in front of them in real-life play situations. They are very ingenious and resourceful at adapting resources. It is not necessary to provide expensive manufactured items. Children will happily take on different parts during role play; they can be both the driver and the passenger on a bus. Younger children often prefer to play solo or with an adult, then as they mature they develop stronger relationships with peers and are keen to join in group play.

Staff discussion

- Be aware that, as a significant adult, you are an important role model and the children will pick up on your behaviour, your language and your values.
- Consider the impact on the child of the very close relationship he forms with his key person. Discuss the importance of any imitation that will arise from this relationship.
- As you engage with babies and young children, ask another member of staff to video or photograph the activity and then reflect on what happened and how it could be extended.

3. Exploring and re-enacting

Young children re-enact familiar scenes with the help of people, props and resources.

*(**Birth to Three Matters**)*

Babies

Babies that have opportunities to explore the world from an early age and express their emotions develop intellectually. They need to be stimulated by a range of experiences that they can react to and interact with. Re-enactment or revisiting an experience gives the baby the opportunity to assimilate and embed ideas. Developing the imagination requires time and space to think and dream and a rich visual environment can encourage this. Look for simple resources, ones that are open ended and can be used in many different ways. Through careful observation a sensitive key person can tune in to a baby's interest and provide support.

Practical activities

- Provide interesting items to hang from a gym frame, such as shiny tin foil cases to kick or reach out to and hold, brightly coloured plastic washing scourers that have a texture to feel.

- Use ballerina netting to create a canopy and place large silk flowers on the top or put the flowers inside a discovery bottle as these are light and can be lifted and held easily by a baby.

- Provide a selection of hats and a safety mirror. Sit with the baby and spend time looking at your reflections and exchanging hats.

- Fit long, fine scarves into transparent plastic tubes or boxes. Demonstrate how to grasp one end and pull the scarf through. As the baby gets older use opaque tubes/boxes so that the scarf seems to disappear and reappear.

- Have a collection of soft brushes, like those used for make-up blusher, for the baby to hold or to stroke her hand. Play music and observe the babies using them freely.

Toddlers

Children's learning begins by observing and imitating the behaviour they see in adults, their siblings and their peers. They re-enact familiar scenes, use props and resources as they practise being grown up. Listen carefully and you will hear them take on different voices and phrases as they pretend to be Mummy or Daddy.

Practical activities

- Provide resources so that children can act out familiar everyday events. Include a range of hats, shoes and bags. Ensure that the home play area is equipped with domestic items and includes those used by a range of cultures.

- Help the children to create simple puppets using socks with eyes and a mouth, paper plates on sticks or finger puppets. Play alongside, positioned at the child's level, and take advantage of natural openings to initiate a dialogue yet talk as partners in the conversation. Make some of the paper plates with faces that show different emotions such as happy, sad or angry to encourage the children to discuss their feelings. Observe how the children respond/talk to the puppet rather than to the adult.

- Create large-scale puppets that an adult can manipulate to introduce language patterns such as greetings and polite conversation. Extend their use to cover manners and positive behaviour.

- Tell the story of *The Tiger Who Came to Tea*. Encourage the children to join in with appropriate words and gestures and act out the story using pretend tea party props. Make an apron with a central flap/opening so you can make the food 'disappear' into the tiger's tummy.

- Set up a café-style snack area where the children can go when they are hungry or thirsty and act out their knowledge of eating out.

- Set up a display of familiar items – real everyday things. Ask the children to select three and make up a story with them including the chosen items as you go. Encourage the children to 'have a go' at making up their own oral stories. They may start with just a few words but with gentle encouragement develop a sequence.

- Tell stories of everyday happenings but personalise them by including the names of the children within the group. Encourage the children to recall and retell their own news.

- Provide resources in the water tray for children to wash dolls. Have sponges, soapy water and towels. Listen to the words they use and observe the care and attention they give to the dolls as they recreate this familiar task. Ask 'Have you washed behind their ears, in between their toes'? Introduce the rhyme 'This little piggy went to market' and other games that parents/carers play with their babies.

Outcomes for the child

- Developing a better understanding of the world and the way that people behave.
- Being positive and confident.
- Developing a disposition to be imaginative.

Focus points

The imagination is stimulated by sights and sounds so check out your collection of music and expand on it. Young children explore materials and situations in their efforts to understand them, assimilate them and develop a sense of security. They may repeatedly explore resources as they try them out, discover how things work and what they can do. Consider items that can be purchased outside of the toy catalogues: look for alternative sources for resources such as haberdashery stores, kitchen departments, garden centres and DIY stores. Use more empty cardboard boxes for imaginative play.

Staff discussion

- How imaginative are we? Encourage staff to support each other as they plan and discuss their activities. Encourage staff to work in pairs, with one imaginative member of staff helping another who feels less able to be imaginative.

- Plan for staff to go and see a live performance, or an exhibition together that has imaginative sections. Having shared the same event, think what could be used in the setting. It may only be the way colour and lights were used to create an atmosphere for example.

4. Sensory

Imaginative opportunities for babies to explore movement and materials which use all the senses, both alone and in a group.

(Birth to Three Matters)

Babies

Once babies become mobile, they move towards anything they see, such as a small scrap of paper or lost label from a soft toy. They are very inquisitive. At around 3–6 months they discover their legs and feet and start kicking. Repeating motor skills over and over again strengthens the neural circuits that go from the brain's thinking areas to the motor areas and then out to the nerves that move muscles.

Early climbing occurs at around 6–9 months. Try placing small obstacles, such as a bolster pillow, in their path and observe if the babies see them as a challenge to push or climb over using their newly found mobility and body movements. Being aware that repetition assists learning, the responsive practitioner needs to provide interesting and imaginative layouts and activities to keep this interest alive.

Practical activities

- Activity frames or gyms that children lie beneath can be a useful tool. Change the hanging items to provide stimulation for a child to kick and reach something new.

- Lie a baby down and hold a thin foil plate for her to kick at. Use gestures and rewarding verbal support to encourage movements.

- Wiggles and shuffles help in the formation of the brain synapses that develop large motor skills. Tummy time – lying a baby down with exciting items in her eye line – will encourage movements. Use real fruit which has colour, texture and temperature and sometimes intriguing smells.

- Rolling over is important and uses chest and arm muscles. Put down a soft mat and lie the baby down. Sing 'One in the bed and the mummy/daddy said roll over' and gently roll the baby over.

- Provide soft fluffy rugs to encourage rolling – roll over yourself and play as you do this.

Toddlers

As young children mature, they begin to use movements and actions to act out internal ideas and try them out them for real. They may repeat certain activities over and over again and in this way, will be laying down the foundation for the development of skills and preparation for future learning. Individual learning styles may begin to emerge such as VAK: Visual, Auditory, Kinaesthetic (touch, movement and emotions), which can indicate a child's sensory preference when taking in and recalling information. Younger toddlers may be happy playing and pretending on their own but may get drawn into co-operative play when attracted by the plan or the idea.

Practical activities

- With a small group, introduce finger rhymes and action songs. For example, mime using a hair brush 'This is the way we brush our hair' or provide a steering wheel for the 'driver' of the bus as you sing 'The wheels on the bus go round and round' and encourage the 'passengers' to join in with the actions.

- Play 'Follow my leader'. The adult initiates the game and then the children take the lead.

- Introduce materials into creative play that have a distinctive texture such as rough-feeling sandpaper, a knobbly gourd, shiny, slippery silver paper or smooth velvet. Draw the children's attention to the feel of the materials and ask them if they like it. Make a textures book or a wall display so that the children can touch them. Repeat this with other sensory materials, for example items that make a noise: 'Can you hear that? What do you think it is?'

- For those children who prefer solitary play provide individual sand trays and a variety of materials, such as lentils, dried peas, gravel and sand, to mix and mould for pretend cooking. Have a selection

Caution: Be vigilant that the children do not put the materials into their mouths.

of patty tins to make pies, chapattis, pizza. At the end of the play let the children sieve the materials into separate containers so that they can be reused.

- Set up an 'Office' area with mark-making materials, any redundant IT (information technology) equipment, phones, files and paper. If possible, allow the children to observe how the adults use their own office equipment so that they have real experience to draw upon.

- For those children who like to play on their own set up a table with a mirror, some hats, necklaces and face paints.

- Toy telephones help young children learn the give and take of conversation. Adults can help by joining in and using conventional greetings: 'Hello. Who's that?' 'How are you?'

- Play movement games with the children that encourage them to move like animals, for example slow and heavy like an elephant, galloping like a horse or slithering like a snake.

- Place some objects in a bag and ask the children to guess what they are. Include items that they have encountered during the day, for example a gourd, and give some simple clues: 'It's round and knobbly...' Let them feel the objects through the bag.

Outcomes for the child

- Developing muscles.
- Developing connectors in the brain.
- Understanding space.
- Developing more control of their body.
- Discovering ways to express emotions and feelings.
- Experimenting and exploring the properties of materials.

Focus points

At times, during pretend play, children may act out scenes that adults find distressing, for example war play, fighting or being drunk. Adults need to interpret these actions very carefully and not be too quick to judge. Children may not be acting out experiences relating to real life but scenes from TV.

Staff discussion

- Do you incorporate a physical session in the baby room, making it imaginative and sensory?

- How would you support, or at what stage would you intervene in, aggressive war play?

- Do you give children sufficient time to let their play evolve and develop? What strategies do you employ to move their play forward?

5. Pretending

Provide materials which encourage young children to pretend without your intervention.

(Birth to Three Matters)

Babies

Safety is of the utmost importance when working with babies so any materials that are provided without adult interaction or intervention need to be treated with caution. For example, careful observation is required when giving a baby a soft hat. It can be pulled inadvertently over the mouth or nose area and this could cause distress, even if breathing is difficult for only a few seconds. Babies love to explore unusual items especially those with textures. Using see-through objects can also be very reassuring as a baby feels that you are still there should she look up for reassurance. A wooden block or massage roller can be many things in a child's imagination and good observational skills by the practitioner are very important. Capture what is happening with photographic evidence and annotated notes to share with parents/carers and colleagues.

Practical activities

- Using soft play mattresses or exercise mats lay out some small teddies or dolls, some cloths and boxes, put one of the toys in a box, half cover another with a cloth. Watch and wait to see what follows and how the toys are used, regrouped, ignored and new play occurs.
- Collect some soft hats and put them near a safety mirror.
- Put out some small plastic bowls, dolls and teddies. Add some small bath sponges and flannels – allow total freedom, watch and see.
- Attach ballerina netting to form a small canopy, leaving the sides open. Inside put some small plastic bottles, balls, and place mats (thin, plastic picnic variety). This provides an early den (environment) – an imaginative zone.

Toddlers

Spontaneous imaginary play can happen anytime, anywhere. All young children need is the space and time. Younger toddlers may enjoy solitary play, developing friendships with an imaginary playmate and having 'conversations' with their toys. However, once they begin to play in a group, they appear to develop a shared understanding of the play 'script', instantly knowing what to do when, where and how. They show initiative beyond their years and ingenuity in developing resources and solving problems.

Practical activities

- Supply materials for making dens and tunnels, indoors or outdoors. This can include crates, strong cardboard boxes, blankets and pegs or bulldog clips to secure them. For a more permanent structure plant willow twigs into the ground then weave them to form natural, living secret spaces.
- Provide resources for shopping play that include small trolleys, counters with a till and 'money', bags, baskets and a variety of goods to 'purchase'. Observe the children's knowledge and understanding of simple transactions, social skills and emerging mathematical language.

- Ensure that young children can access play materials easily and safely. Store small world toys in transparent containers at child height. Supply non-slip mats or trays where the children can set out their own scenes and develop their imaginative play independently.

- Block play needs space and it can often spread throughout the room. If situated near to the home play area, the blocks can be used to complement and extend the children's ideas.

- Display dressing-up clothes attractively and on hangers. Change them frequently and add extra pieces. Include clothing from a range of cultures, items that denote a profession, such as a postman's hat and bag, a chef's hat and apron. Include a workman's belt with tools and a hard hat. Link the dressing-up clothes to any special interest or celebration, for example wedding dresses or a 'dragon's mask'. Have lengths of material (silk, cotton or velvet) for the children to use according to their imagination and the needs of the moment.

Outcomes for the child

- Developing independence and self-confidence.
- Forming relationships and friendships.
- Being allowed to have a 'flow' of learning which is unbroken allows concentration skills to develop.
- Sustaining play and achieving a feeling of pleasure within play.

Focus points

Free play is child initiated and does not always need any input from an adult. Young children give clear signals that they are playing. Their gestures and facial expressions say 'this is not serious, it's fun'. They over-act, using extravagant movements, they get noisy, exuberant, smiling, even screaming. Conflict is an integral part of the script and is usually resolved peaceably so that it doesn't stop the play. The adults' role is to supply materials that help to stimulate the play and at times to move it forward. However, they need to balance their intervention carefully so that the free play remains child initiated not adult directed.

Staff discussion

- How can you convey to children that you value their spontaneous play?

- Notice if one group is taking over certain play resources, for example the blocks or wheeled toys. What could you do to rectify this?

- Do you have a system for carrying out spot checks on the state of equipment that the children are using? Are broken resources replaced or repaired?

6. Expressing

Adults who play and talk with children and who encourage them to express themselves imaginatively.

(Birth to Three Matters)

Babies

Babies love the engagement of an interested adult who is flexible and is not afraid to play! Eye contact, making sounds and singing are an essential part of the toolkit of an effective practitioner who works with babies. By being imaginative yourself you can allow babies to see that anything goes and the world of the imagination is a wonderful escape.

Babies have been known to look at an adult who is trying to direct play blankly as if to say 'does it have to *be* something?' Being part of play requires commitment from the adult. A practitioner should not be the director of play but rather the enabler, or the imitator. Developing babies' imagination means engagement of a sophisticated nature. Babies need to feel it is wonderful to be imaginative. The value placed on this is very important.

Communication with babies in terms of gestures and facial expressions is an important part of engaging in an imaginative time. Expressing imagination evolves through physical movement, sounds, mark making and creative play.

Practical activities

- Provide some 'what's inside?' toys – this element of the unknown allows freedom of thought and imagination. Collect small boxes and baskets and put in different things each day so that babies are trained to wonder.

- Provide a treasure basket called 'I wonder' – put objects in this like gourds, butter squash, lengths of see-through cloths, pine-cones, pegs, items with holes in to look through such as spaghetti measures.

- Use plastic mirror tiles for displays or put several on a piece of board and place the dolls and teddies on this – with plates and cups.

- Share a book with a baby and then collect some of the items in the book as a prop. Add to these an interesting surface such as a bamboo or fluffy rug and some boxes and watch and interact appropriately with the play.

Toddlers

Young children experience many new emotions but have not developed the language skills to express what they are feeling. During spontaneous imaginative play, they can take on a role and release some of their emotions through the character's voice. They can express fear, excitement and anger. Structured imaginative play and sensitive discussion can help to provide a role model of behaviour where the children can work through their emotions.

Practical activities

- Use traditional stories and rhymes, such as 'Humpty Dumpty', 'Little Miss Muffet' or 'Goldilocks and the three bears' to promote a discussion about feelings. Encourage the children to join in with the repetitive phrases. Stop and ask 'What will happen next?' 'Why was Humpty sitting on the wall? Did he fall or was he pushed?' 'Why did Miss Muffet run away from the spider?' 'Should Goldilocks have gone into the bears' cottage?'

- Plan positive and happy experiences such as a treasure hunt. Hide objects and discover simple clues that lead on to the next one until the treasure is found. Make sure the 'treasure' can be enjoyed by the whole group. Read *Rosie's Walk* by Pat Hutchins.

- Develop a wide range of music for the children to access freely that covers different emotions – peaceful and tranquil, happy and joyful, marching music, dancing and whirling.

- Provide opportunities for vigorous outdoor play where children can 'let off steam'. Set up a row of saucepan lids and clay flower pots that can be hit with a spoon or a child-sized spade for 'furious digging'.

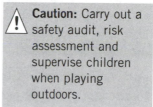

Caution: Carry out a safety audit, risk assessment and supervise children when playing outdoors.

- Have clay or dough that can be squeezed, pummelled and eventually shaped.

- Create an area where children can play quietly with sand and water.

- Create a sound effects tape that tells a simple story. It might include crunchy footsteps, a gate slamming, an ice-cream van signal. Talk about their thoughts and feelings as they listened to the tape.

- Record the children during the day and play back at the end of the session. Do they remember what happened?

Outcomes for the child

- Growing sense of self-awareness and control.
- Receiving positive feedback encourages further development of the imagination.
- Begin to understand what is/is not acceptable behaviour.
- Aware that others have feelings.
- Thinking creatively encourages 'thinking outside of the box'.
- Losing yourself in your imagination is pleasurable and soothing.

Focus points

The role of the practitioner is vital in helping young children come to terms with complex, new and difficult emotions. During these early years they may be feeling anger, grief, jealousy, pride, embarrassment, rejection, even guilt, and yet do not have the language to express what is wrong. They resolve this by biting, fighting, storming off, sulking. Once they have learnt to control these emotions they are more likely to be accepted by their peers and make secure friendships. The adult can help young children express their feelings by naming and acknowledging them and by providing appropriate imaginative play experiences. Inventors and artists could not operate without the use of their imaginations. The imagination cannot operate in a 'controlled' environment; there needs to be stimulation and excitement injected into the environment in order for the imagination to flourish.

Staff discussion

- Discuss how your setting encourages children's imaginations. Start the staff discussion with a practical, open-ended task that is fun.
- Talk about what you know about the 'imagination'. Ask staff to bring one interesting fact or piece of information from books, the internet, a professional magazine, to get them thinking about this important area of learning.
- How do you judge when to intervene and when to 'back off'?
- What can you do to promote well-being?
- Explore strategies that may help children overcome loss, such as acting out through toys and dolls, drawing/painting and relevant stories.

References

Adams, S. and Moyles, J. (2005) *Images of Violence: Responding to Children's Representations of the Violence They See*. Lutterworth: Featherstone Education.

Ahlberg, A. and Ahlberg, J. (1999) *The Jolly Postman, or Other People's Letters*. New York: Viking Kestrel Picture Books.

Berenstain, S. and Berenstain, J. (1985) *The Berenstain Bears Forget Their Manners*. London: Random House.

DfES (Department for Education and Skills) (2002) *Birth to Three Matters: A Framework to Support Children in their Earliest Years*. London: DfES.

DfES (Department for Education and Skills) (2003) *Every Child Matters*. London: DfES.

DfES (Department for Education and Skills)/DWP (Department for Work and Pensions) (2003) *National Standards for Under 8s Day Care and Childminding (Full Day Care)*. London: DfES.

Gretz, S. (1986) *It's Your Turn Roger*. London: Picture Lions.

Gussin Paley, V. (1984) *Boys and Girls: Superheroes in the Doll Corner*. Chicago, IL: University of Chicago Press.

Kerr, J. (2006) *The Tiger Who Came to Tea*. London: HarperCollins.

Moyles, J. (1989) *Just Playing: The Role and Status of Play in Early Childhood Education*. Milton Keynes: Open University Press.

Rogers, A. (1990) *Superheroes and War Play in Preschool: Let Them In or Lock Them Out*. Detroit, MI: Ypsilanti High/Scope Press.

Rosen, M. (2005) *We're Going on a Bear Hunt*. London: Walker Books.

Scarry, R. (1973) *Please and Thank You Book*. London: Random House Pictureback.

Yolen, J. (2005) *How Do Dinosaurs Eat Their Food?* New York: Scholastic.

Resources

Safety mirrors, made from acrylic, can be purchased from educational suppliers and DIY stores. Camouflage nets can be sourced from Army Stores or the internet.

Conclusion

The spark is responsible for the fire but without air and tinder there would be no flame
Mihaly Csikszentmihalyi 1996

In order for children to become competent learners, they need a combination of factors that include all four aspects of this book: connecting, imagining, creating, representing to shape the way they understand the world and see themselves in it. Even as adults our perceptions are changing and adjusting as we have new experiences, our senses constantly monitor and adapt to new situations and circumstances. Young children have unique first moments as they encounter new experiences and ideas. The role of the adult is an important factor in identifying, responding to, and extending those things that a child can nearly do by himself. For as Vygotsky tells us, 'Never teach a child something they can learn by themselves'

- Representation is an important way through which thinking develops; children develop symbolic forms and other ways of representing their thinking such as modelling, drawing, painting, mark making, oral stories and role playing.
- Each child has its own unique way of representing its own interests, needs and strengths.
- Creativity is complex yet satisfying and does not need to have an 'end product'.
- Spontaneous, imaginative play allows children to organise and control their world.

Through careful observation, adults can assess children's competencies and their individual needs. They can discover what a child can do and build upon that by providing a wide range of experiences and materials rather than trying to move children from one level to the next. It is not only the child who needs to be a competent learner, they need to be with adults who recognise the need from continuing self development, who are well informed, who reflect on their provision and are committed to delivering quality.

Picasso once said, 'Once I drew very well just like Raphael, but it has taken all my life to know how to draw like a five year old child'

References

Csikzentmihalyi, M. (1996) *Creativity*. New York: Harper Collins.

Appendix: The Birth to Three Framework for 'A Competent Learner'

A Competent Learner

Making Connections

Connecting ideas and understanding the world

Including
- Making connections through the senses and movement
- Finding out about the environment and other people
- Becoming playfully engaged and involved
- Making patterns, comparing, categorising, classifying

Being Imaginative

Responding to the world imaginatively

Including
- Imitating, mirroring, moving, imagining
- Exploring and re-enacting
- Playing imaginatively with materials using all the senses
- Pretend play with gestures and actions, feelings and relationships, ideas and words

Being Creative

Responding to the world creatively

Including
- Exploring and discovering
- Experimenting with sound, other media and movement
- Developing competence and creativity
- Being resourceful

Representing

Responding to the world with marks and symbols

Including
- Exploring, experimenting and playing
- Discovering that one thing can stand for another
- Creating and experimenting with one's own symbols and marks
- Recognising that others may use marks differently

© DfES/Sure Start (2005) *Birth to Three Matters: An Introduction to the Framework*